STAR WARS®

THE CLONE WARS™

SHIPYARDS OF DOOM

DESIGNER **KRYSTAL HENNES**

ASSISTANT EDITOR **FREDDYE LINS**

ASSOCIATE EDITOR **DAVE MARSHALL**

EDITOR **RANDY STRADLEY**

PUBLISHER **MIKE RICHARDSON**

Special thanks to Elaine Mederer, Jann Moorhead, David Anderman, Leland Chee, Sue Rostoni, and Carol Roeder at Lucas Licensing.

Published by Dark Horse Books, a division of Dark Horse Comics, Inc.
10956 SE Main Street, Milwaukie, OR 97222

darkhorse.com | starwars.com

To find a comics shop in your area, call the Comic Shop Locator Service toll-free at 1.888.266.4226
First edition: September 2008 | ISBN 978-1-59582-207-9

10 9 8 7 6 5 4 3 2
Printed in China

The events in these stories take place sometime during the Clone Wars.

STAR WARS: THE CLONE WARS—SHIPYARDS OF DOOM

THE CLONE WARS™

SHIPYARDS OF DOOM

SCRIPT **HENRY GILROY**   ART **THE FILLBACH BROTHERS**

COLORS **RONDA PATTISON**   LETTERING **MICHAEL HEISLER**

COVER ART **SCOTT HEPBURN**

DARK HORSE BOOKS®

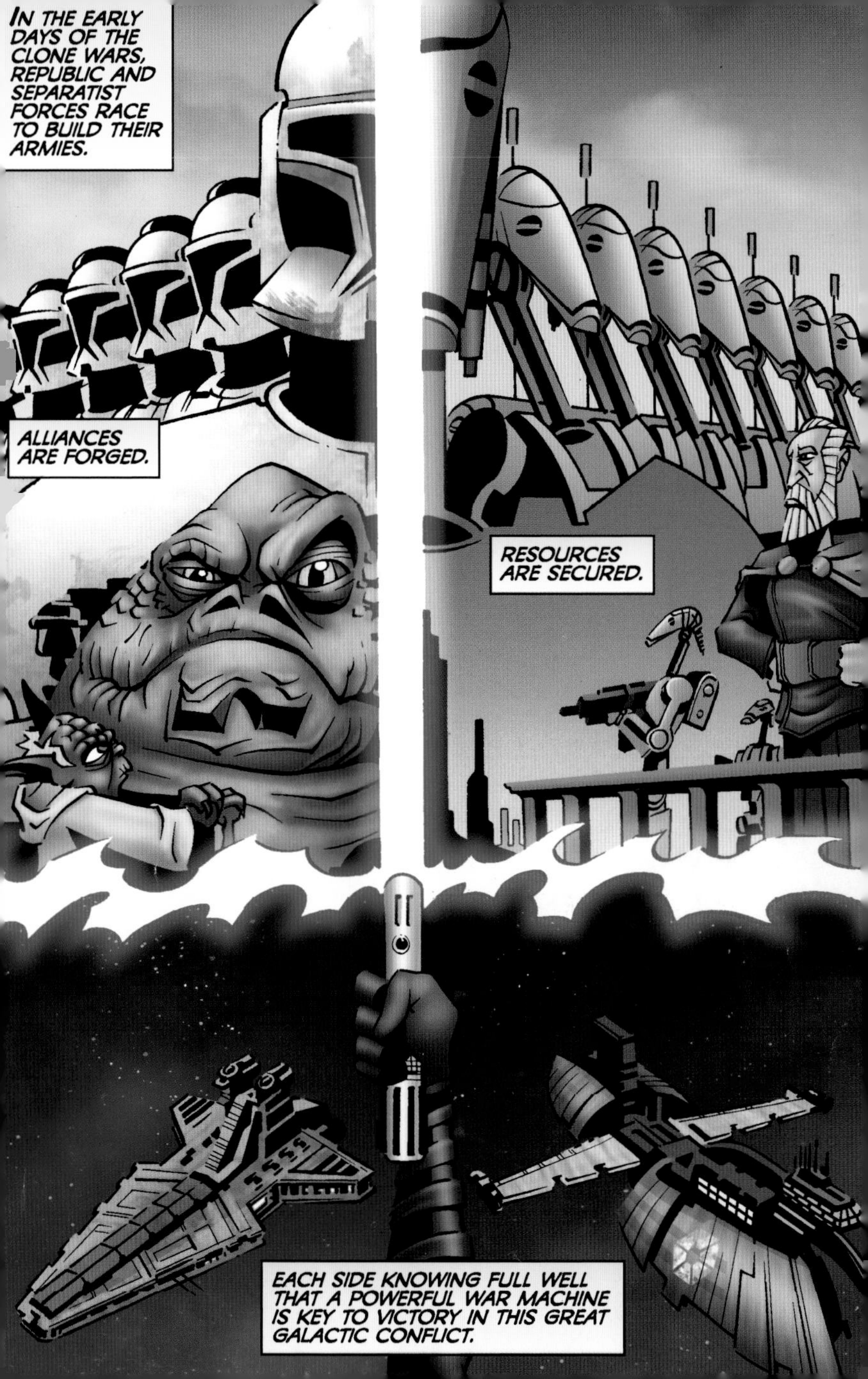
IN THE EARLY DAYS OF THE CLONE WARS, REPUBLIC AND SEPARATIST FORCES RACE TO BUILD THEIR ARMIES.
ALLIANCES ARE FORGED.
RESOURCES ARE SECURED.
EACH SIDE KNOWING FULL WELL THAT A POWERFUL WAR MACHINE IS KEY TO VICTORY IN THIS GREAT GALACTIC CONFLICT.

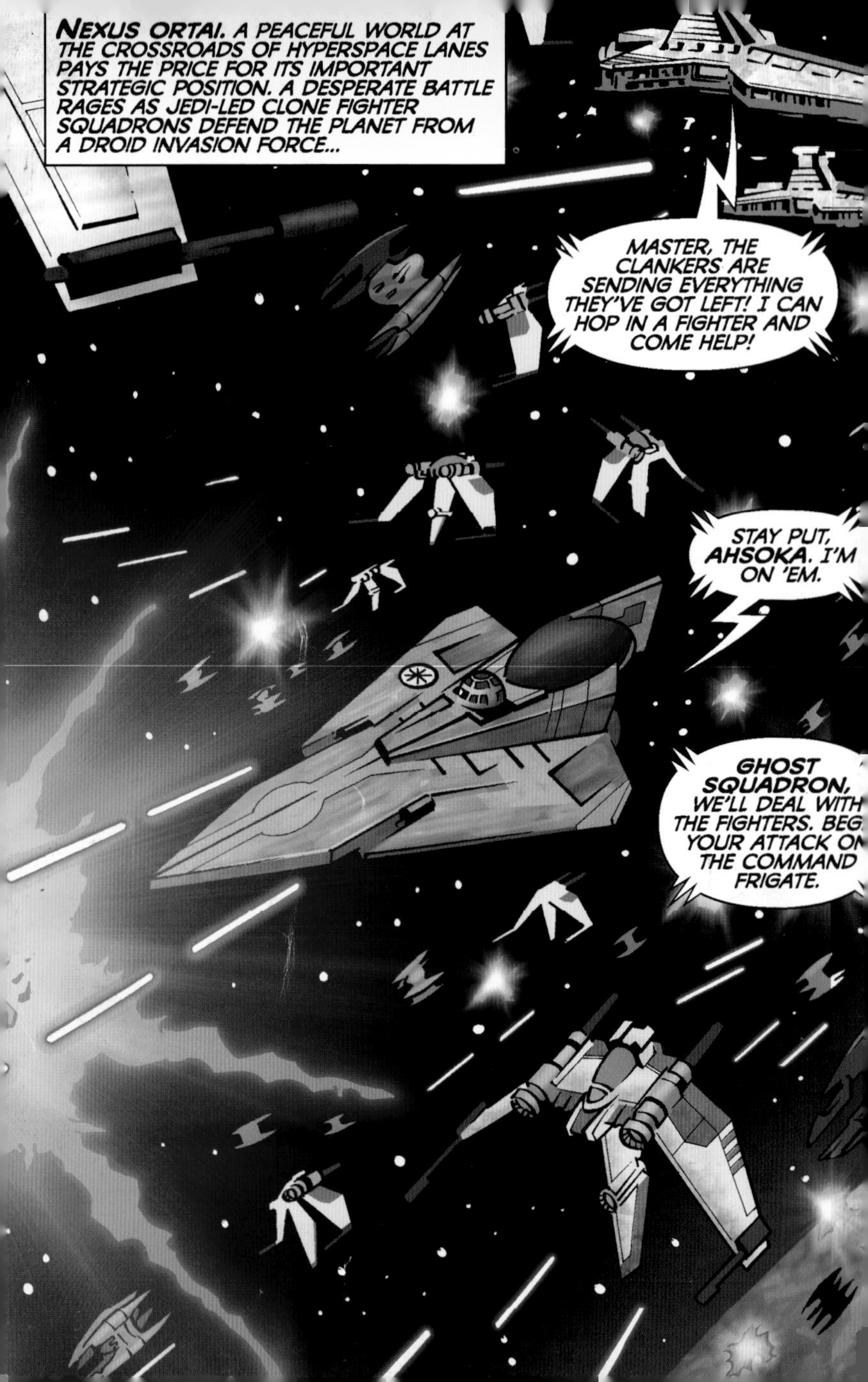
NEXUS ORTAI. A PEACEFUL WORLD AT THE CROSSROADS OF HYPERSPACE LANES PAYS THE PRICE FOR ITS IMPORTANT STRATEGIC POSITION. A DESPERATE BATTLE RAGES AS JEDI-LED CLONE FIGHTER SQUADRONS DEFEND THE PLANET FROM A DROID INVASION FORCE...
MASTER, THE CLANKERS ARE SENDING EVERYTHING THEY'VE GOT LEFT! I CAN HOP IN A FIGHTER AND COME HELP!
STAY PUT, AHSOKA. I'M ON 'EM.
GHOST SQUADRON, WE'LL DEAL WITH THE FIGHTERS. BEG YOUR ATTACK ON THE COMMAND FRIGATE.

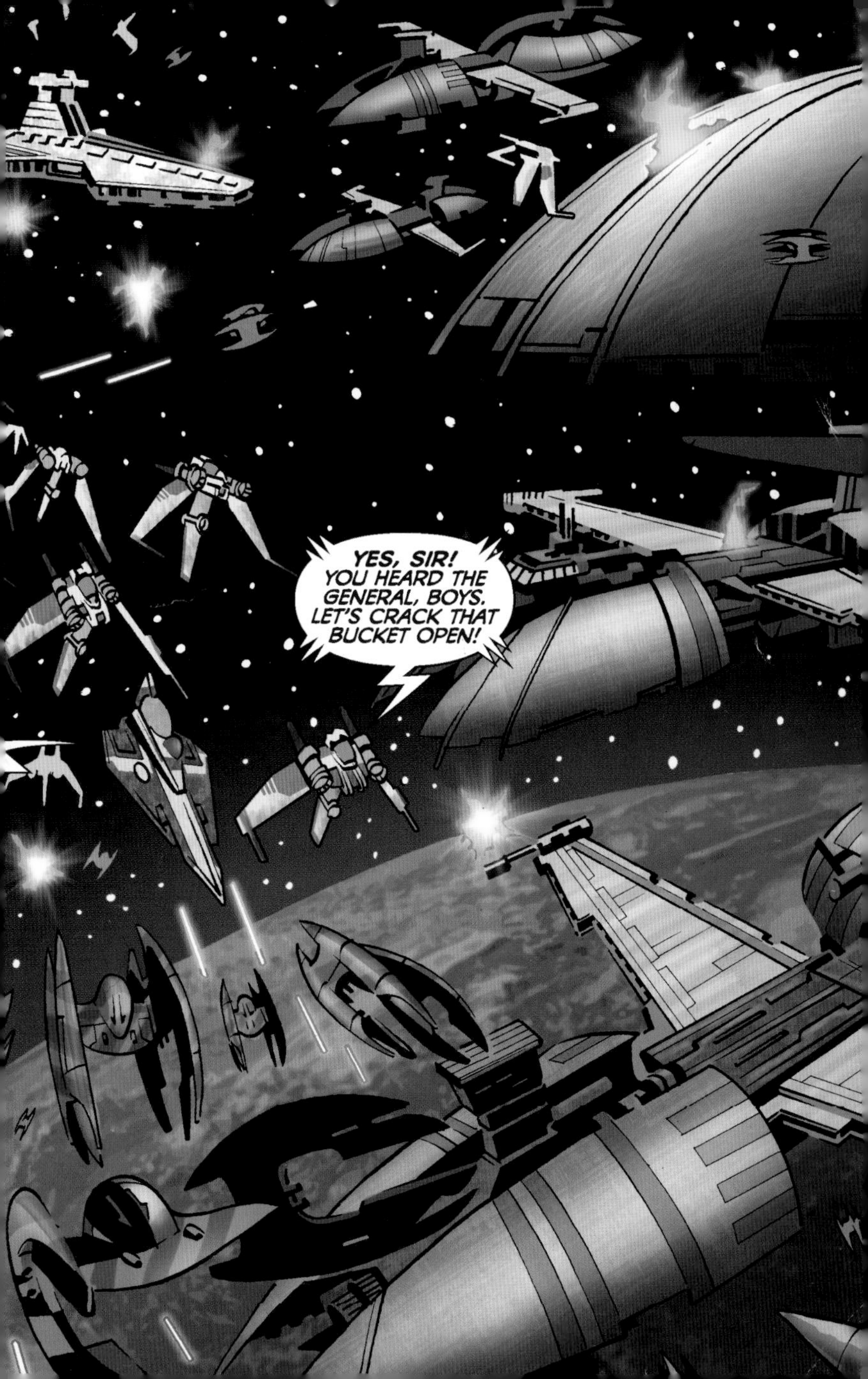
YES, SIR! YOU HEARD THE GENERAL, BOYS. LET'S CRACK THAT BUCKET OPEN!

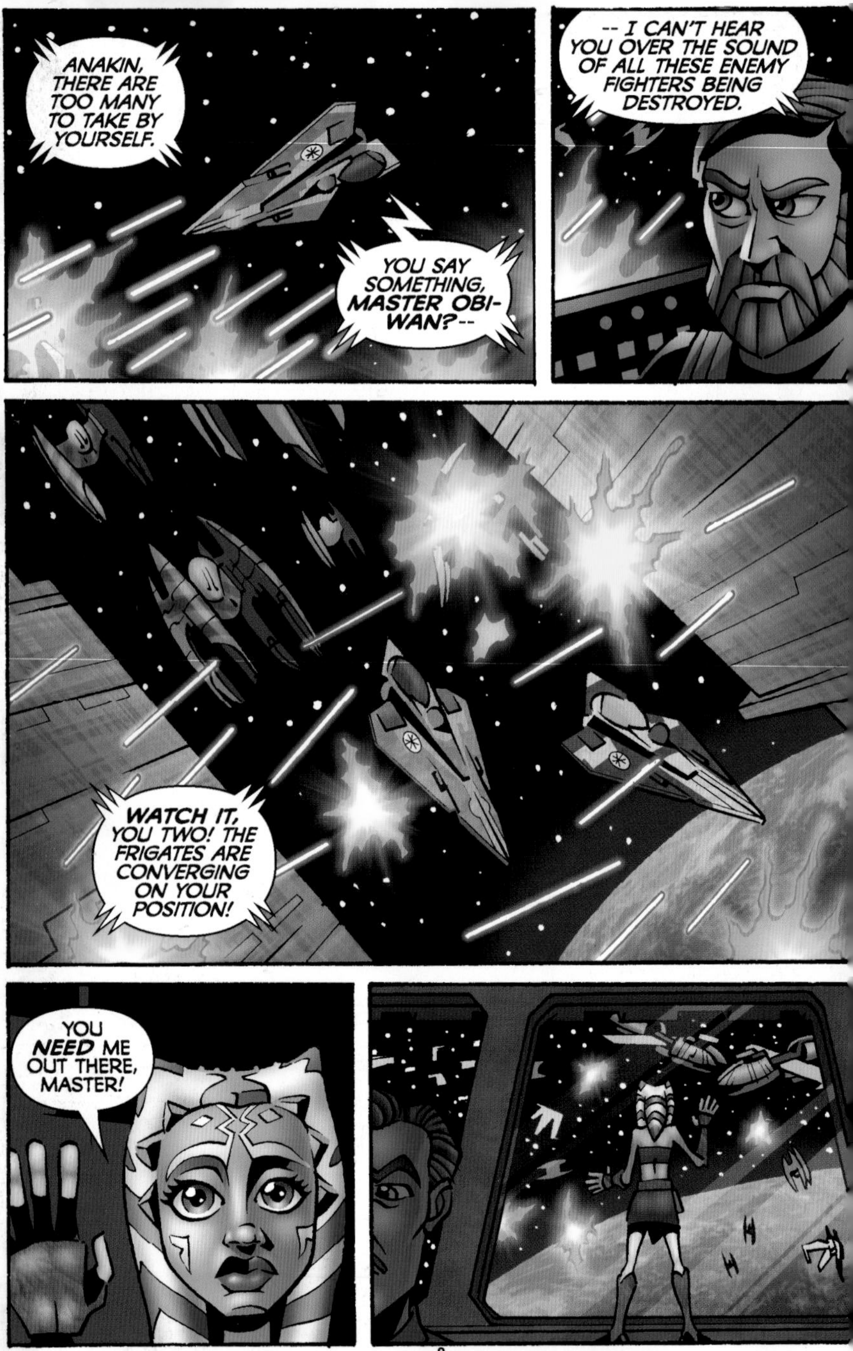
ANAKIN, THERE ARE TOO MANY TO TAKE BY YOURSELF.
YOU SAY SOMETHING, MASTER OBI-WAN?--
-- I CAN'T HEAR YOU OVER THE SOUND OF ALL THESE ENEMY FIGHTERS BEING DESTROYED.
WATCH IT, YOU TWO! THE FRIGATES ARE CONVERGING ON YOUR POSITION!
YOU NEED ME OUT THERE, MASTER!

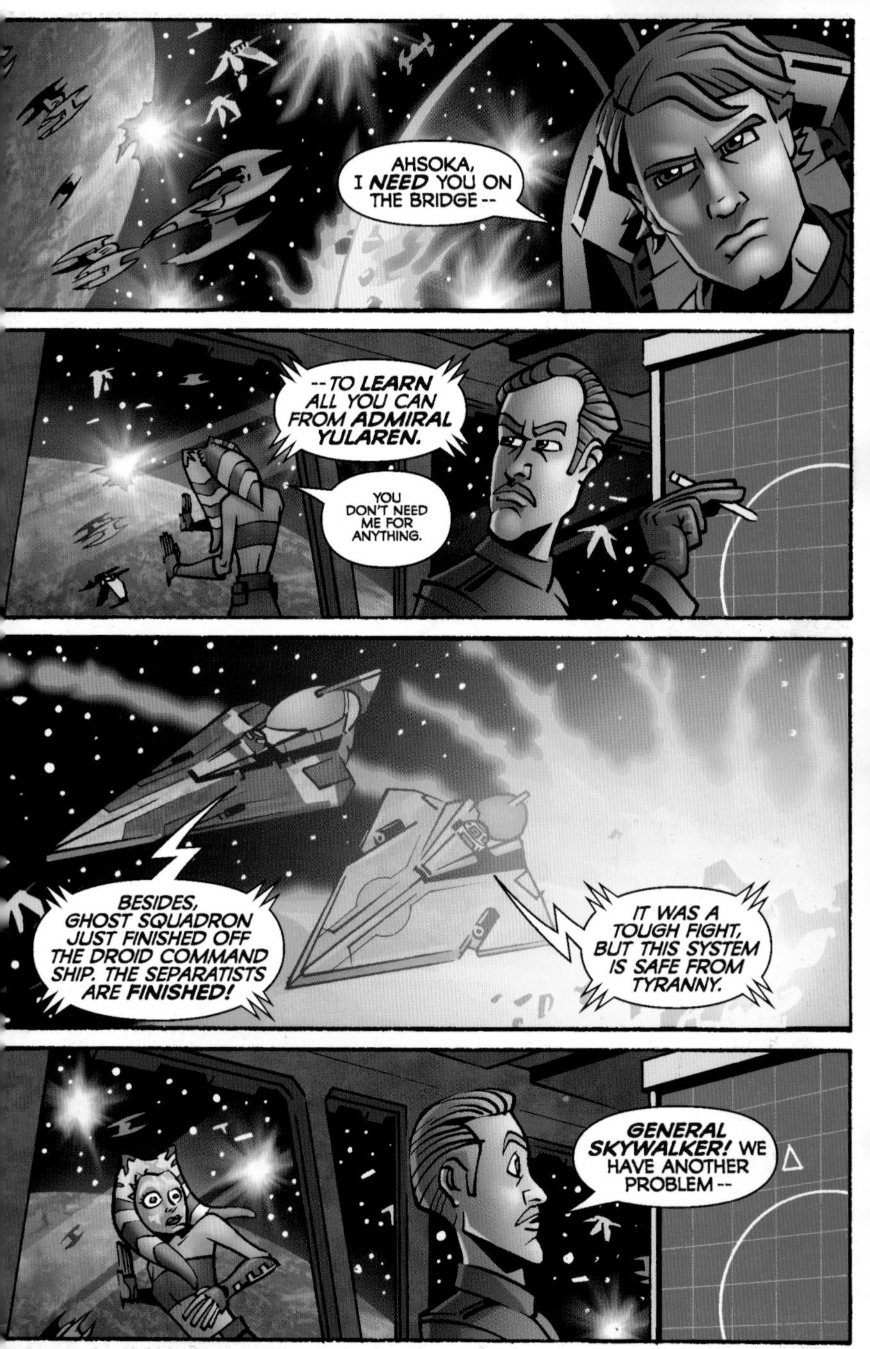
AHSOKA, I NEED YOU ON THE BRIDGE --
--TO LEARN ALL YOU CAN FROM ADMIRAL YULAREN.
YOU DON'T NEED ME FOR ANYTHING.
BESIDES, GHOST SQUADRON JUST FINISHED OFF THE DROID COMMAND SHIP. THE SEPARATISTS ARE FINISHED!
IT WAS A TOUGH FIGHT, BUT THIS SYSTEM IS SAFE FROM TYRANNY.
GENERAL SKYWALKER! WE HAVE ANOTHER PROBLEM --

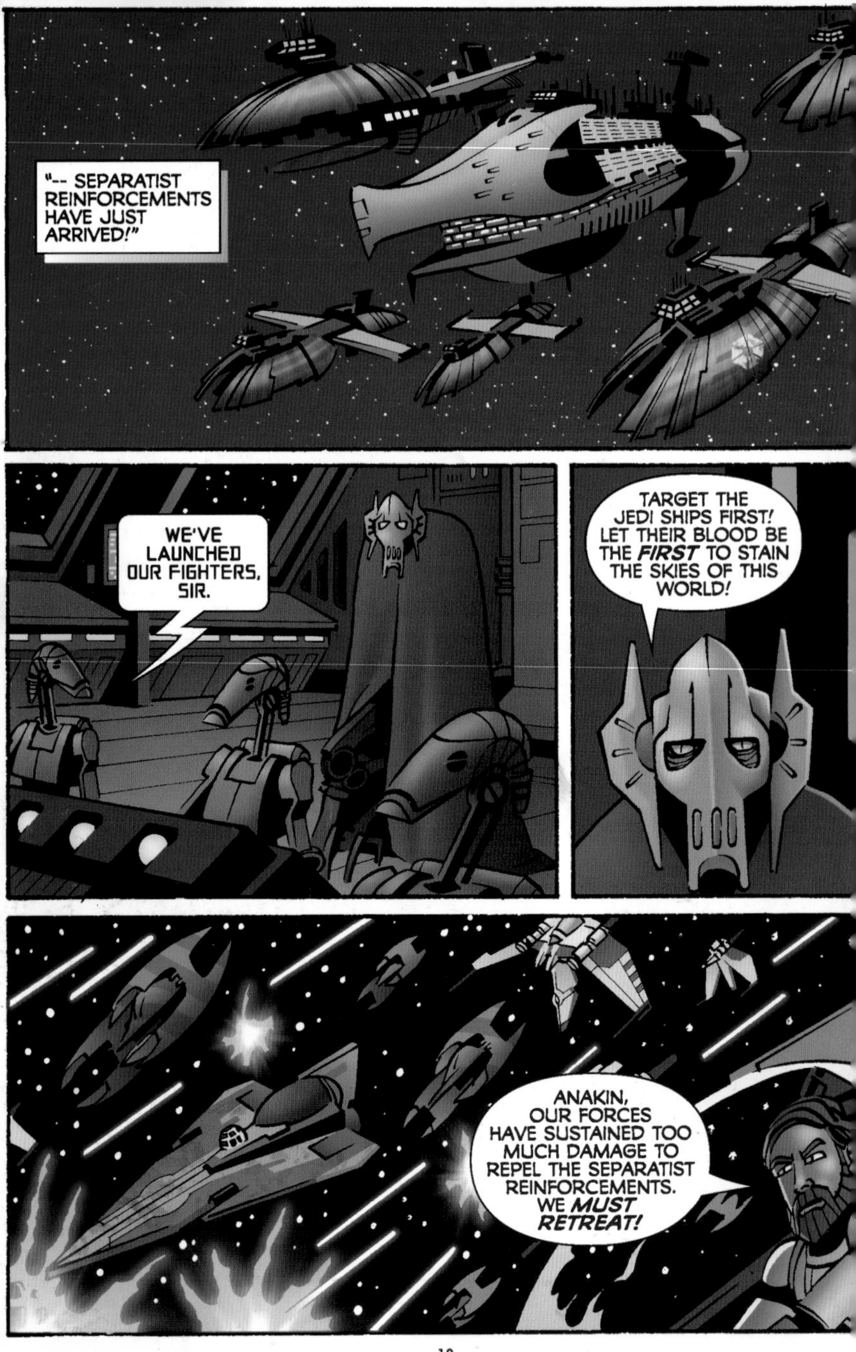
"-- SEPARATIST REINFORCEMENTS HAVE JUST ARRIVED!"
WE'VE LAUNCHED OUR FIGHTERS, SIR.
TARGET THE JEDI SHIPS FIRST! LET THEIR BLOOD BE THE *FIRST* TO STAIN THE SKIES OF THIS WORLD!
ANAKIN, OUR FORCES HAVE SUSTAINED TOO MUCH DAMAGE TO REPEL THE SEPARATIST REINFORCEMENTS. WE *MUST RETREAT!*

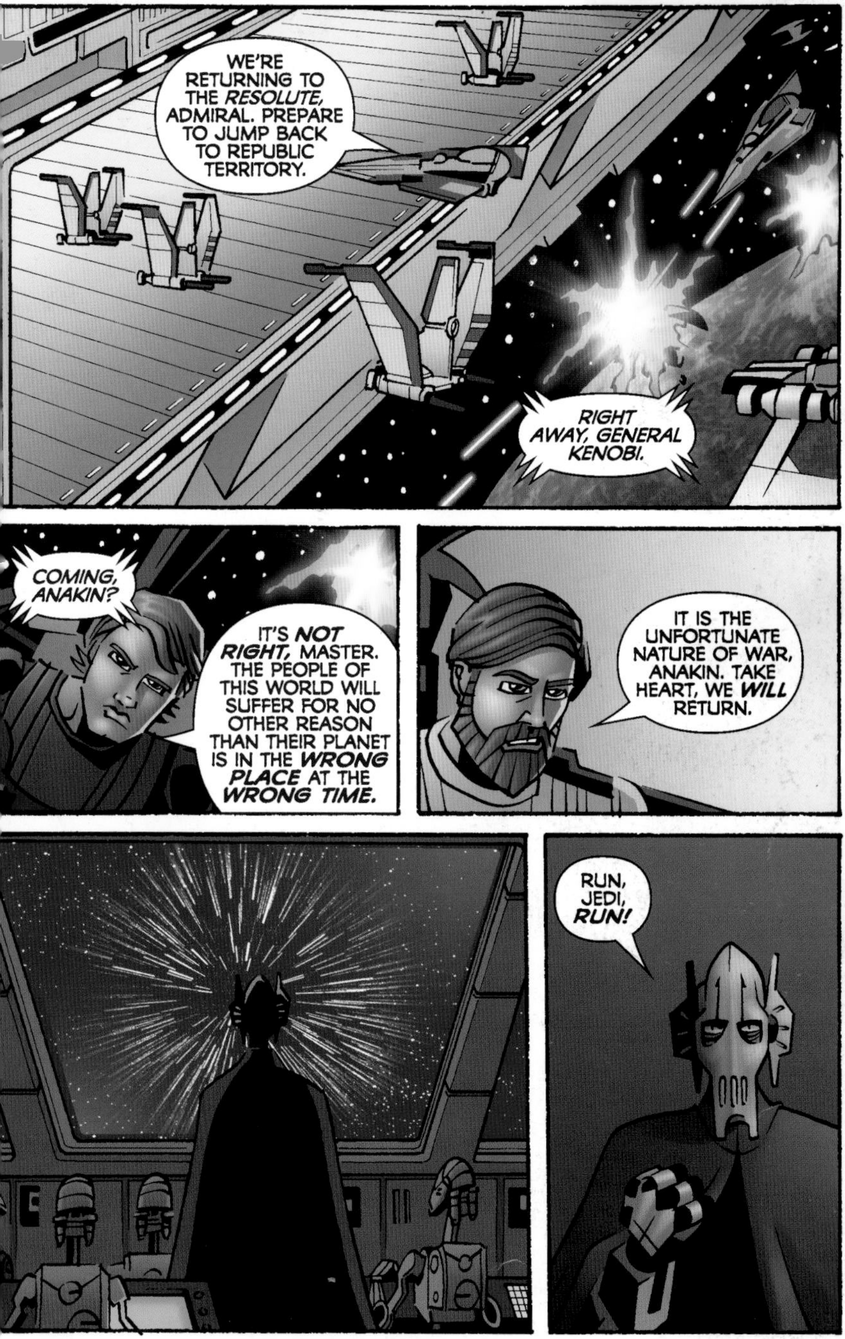
WE'RE RETURNING TO THE *RESOLUTE,* ADMIRAL. PREPARE TO JUMP BACK TO REPUBLIC TERRITORY.
RIGHT AWAY, GENERAL KENOBI.
COMING, ANAKIN?
IT'S ***NOT RIGHT,*** MASTER. THE PEOPLE OF THIS WORLD WILL SUFFER FOR NO OTHER REASON THAN THEIR PLANET IS IN THE ***WRONG PLACE*** AT THE ***WRONG TIME.***
IT IS THE UNFORTUNATE NATURE OF WAR, ANAKIN. TAKE HEART, WE ***WILL*** RETURN.
RUN, JEDI, ***RUN!***

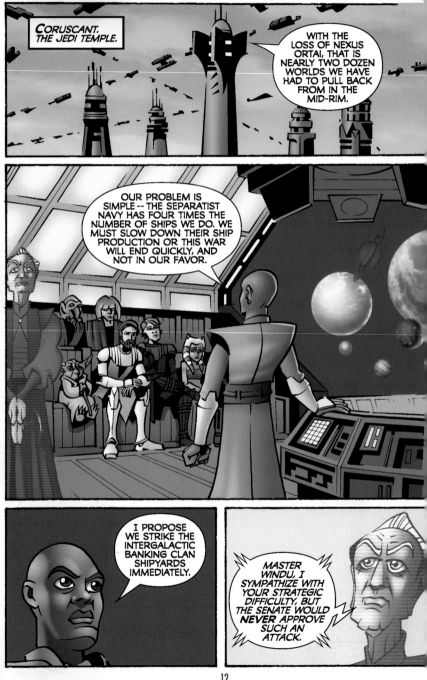

CORUSCANT.
THE JEDI TEMPLE.

WITH THE LOSS OF NEXUS ORTAI, THAT IS NEARLY TWO DOZEN WORLDS WE HAVE HAD TO PULL BACK FROM IN THE MID-RIM.

OUR PROBLEM IS SIMPLE -- THE SEPARATIST NAVY HAS FOUR TIMES THE NUMBER OF SHIPS WE DO. WE MUST SLOW DOWN THEIR SHIP PRODUCTION OR THIS WAR WILL END QUICKLY, AND NOT IN OUR FAVOR.

I PROPOSE WE STRIKE THE INTERGALACTIC BANKING CLAN SHIPYARDS IMMEDIATELY.

MASTER WINDU, I SYMPATHIZE WITH YOUR STRATEGIC DIFFICULTY, BUT THE SENATE WOULD *NEVER* APPROVE SUCH AN ATTACK.

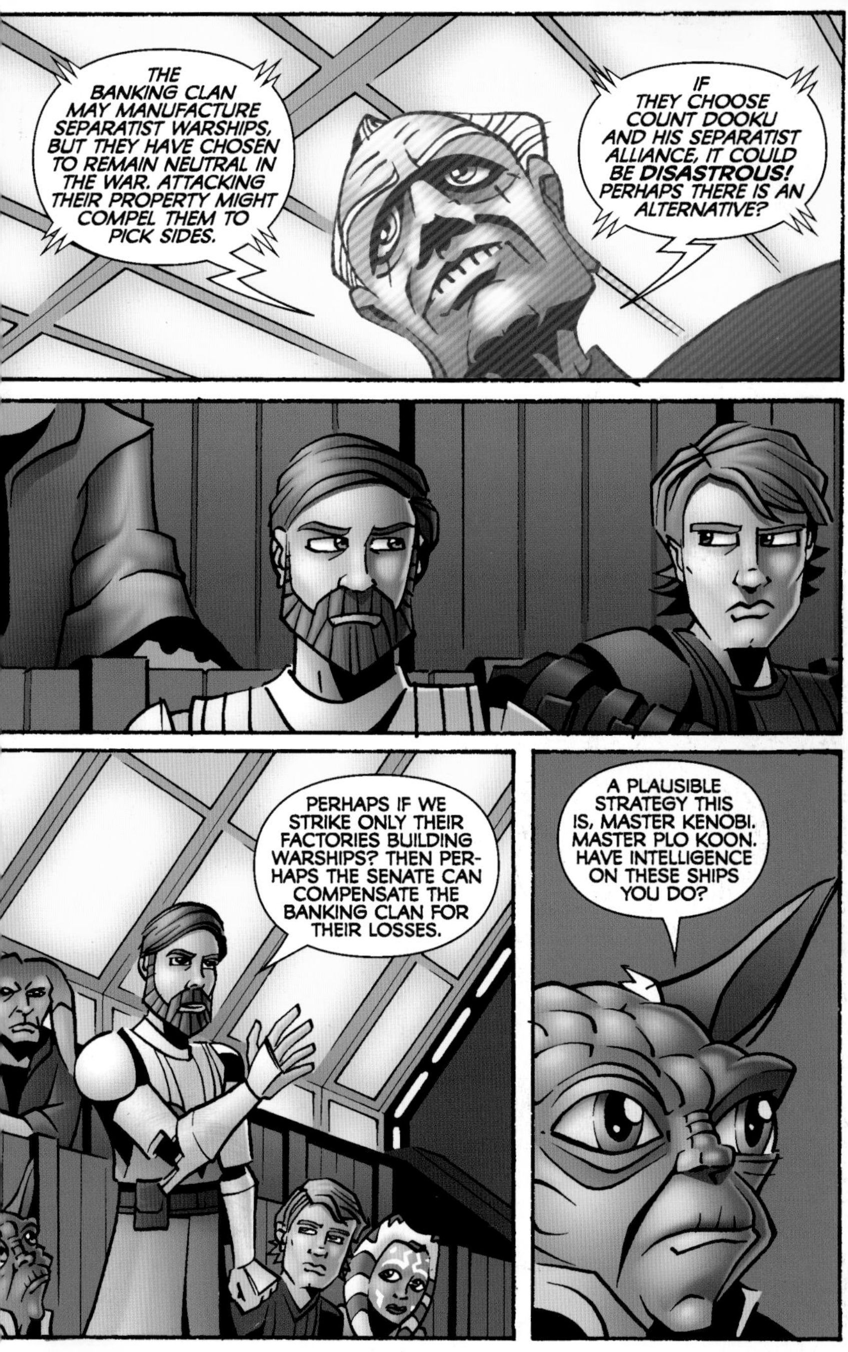
THE BANKING CLAN MAY MANUFACTURE SEPARATIST WARSHIPS, BUT THEY HAVE CHOSEN TO REMAIN NEUTRAL IN THE WAR. ATTACKING THEIR PROPERTY MIGHT COMPEL THEM TO PICK SIDES.
IF THEY CHOOSE COUNT DOOKU AND HIS SEPARATIST ALLIANCE, IT COULD BE **DISASTROUS!** PERHAPS THERE IS AN ALTERNATIVE?
PERHAPS IF WE STRIKE ONLY THEIR FACTORIES BUILDING WARSHIPS? THEN PERHAPS THE SENATE CAN COMPENSATE THE BANKING CLAN FOR THEIR LOSSES.
A PLAUSIBLE STRATEGY THIS IS, MASTER KENOBI. MASTER PLO KOON. HAVE INTELLIGENCE ON THESE SHIPS YOU DO?

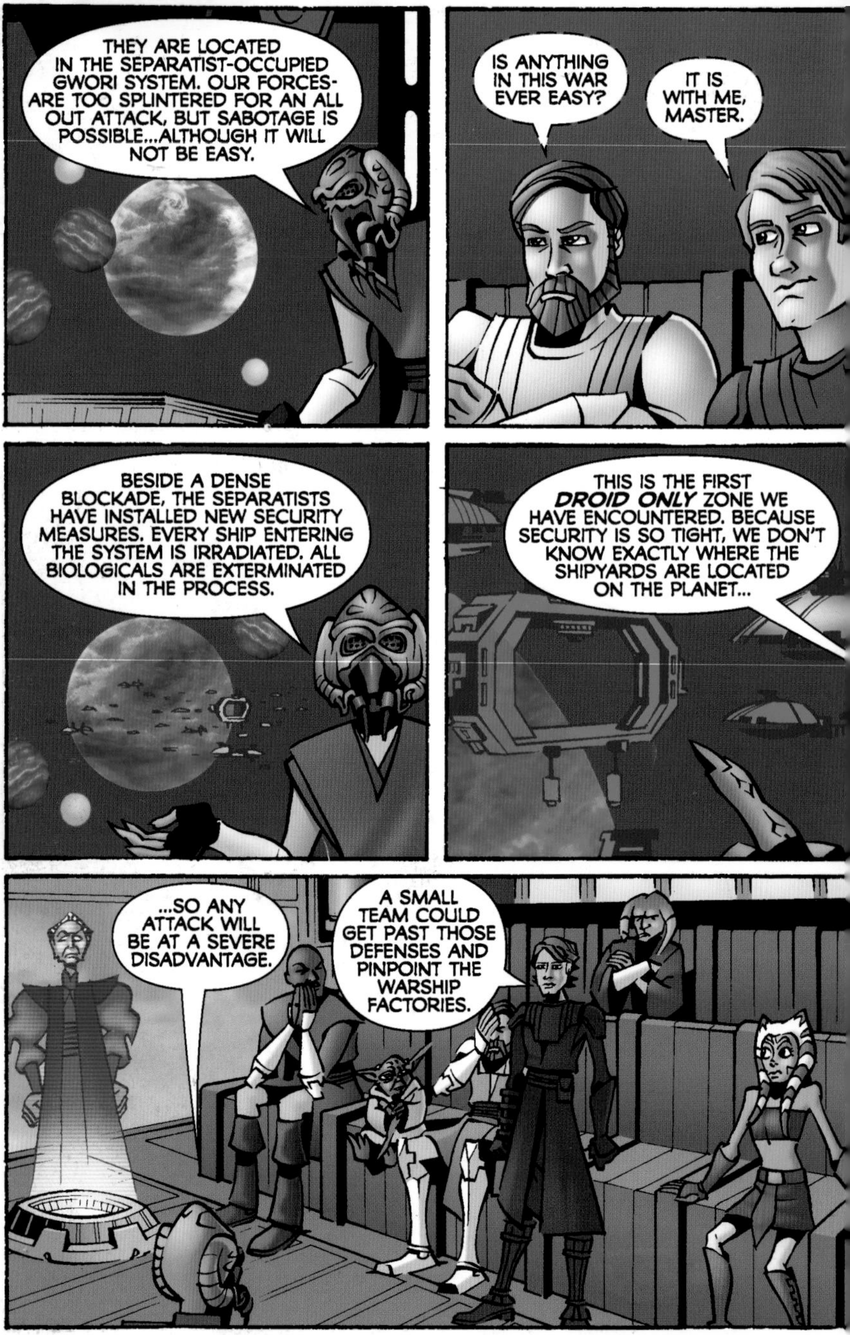
THEY ARE LOCATED IN THE SEPARATIST-OCCUPIED GWORI SYSTEM. OUR FORCES ARE TOO SPLINTERED FOR AN ALL OUT ATTACK, BUT SABOTAGE IS POSSIBLE...ALTHOUGH IT WILL NOT BE EASY.
IS ANYTHING IN THIS WAR EVER EASY?
IT IS WITH ME, MASTER.
BESIDE A DENSE BLOCKADE, THE SEPARATISTS HAVE INSTALLED NEW SECURITY MEASURES. EVERY SHIP ENTERING THE SYSTEM IS IRRADIATED. ALL BIOLOGICALS ARE EXTERMINATED IN THE PROCESS.
THIS IS THE FIRST *DROID ONLY* ZONE WE HAVE ENCOUNTERED. BECAUSE SECURITY IS SO TIGHT, WE DON'T KNOW EXACTLY WHERE THE SHIPYARDS ARE LOCATED ON THE PLANET...
...SO ANY ATTACK WILL BE AT A SEVERE DISADVANTAGE.
A SMALL TEAM COULD GET PAST THOSE DEFENSES AND PINPOINT THE WARSHIP FACTORIES.

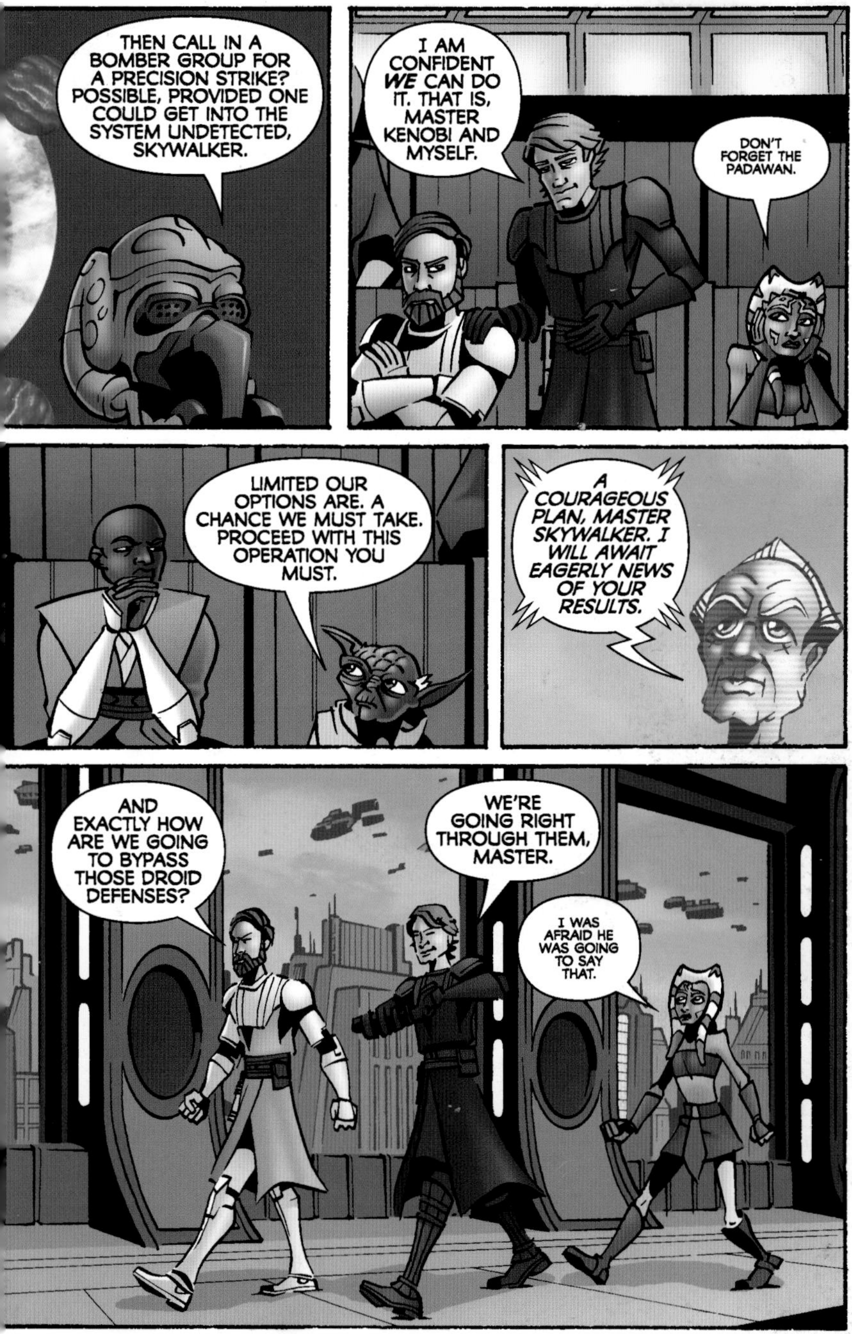
THEN CALL IN A BOMBER GROUP FOR A PRECISION STRIKE? POSSIBLE, PROVIDED ONE COULD GET INTO THE SYSTEM UNDETECTED, SKYWALKER.
I AM CONFIDENT *WE* CAN DO IT. THAT IS, MASTER KENOBI AND MYSELF.
DON'T FORGET THE PADAWAN.
LIMITED OUR OPTIONS ARE. A CHANCE WE MUST TAKE. PROCEED WITH THIS OPERATION YOU MUST.
A COURAGEOUS PLAN, MASTER SKYWALKER. I WILL AWAIT EAGERLY NEWS OF YOUR RESULTS.
AND EXACTLY HOW ARE WE GOING TO BYPASS THOSE DROID DEFENSES?
WE'RE GOING RIGHT THROUGH THEM, MASTER.
I WAS AFRAID HE WAS GOING TO SAY THAT.

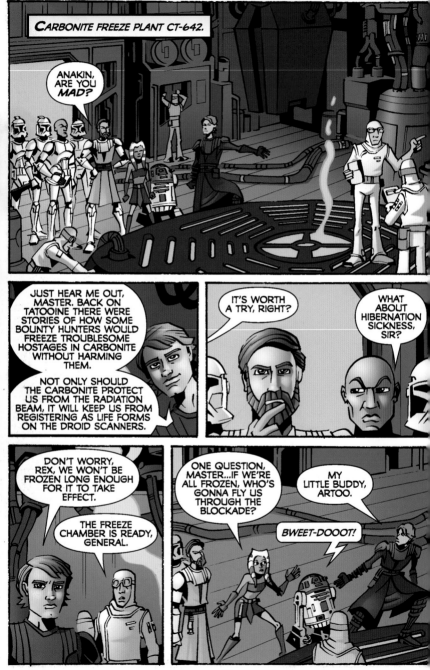

CARBONITE FREEZE PLANT CT-642.

ANAKIN, ARE YOU *MAD*?

JUST HEAR ME OUT, MASTER. BACK ON TATOOINE THERE WERE STORIES OF HOW SOME BOUNTY HUNTERS WOULD FREEZE TROUBLESOME HOSTAGES IN CARBONITE WITHOUT HARMING THEM.

NOT ONLY SHOULD THE CARBONITE PROTECT US FROM THE RADIATION BEAM, IT WILL KEEP US FROM REGISTERING AS LIFE FORMS ON THE DROID SCANNERS.

IT'S WORTH A TRY, RIGHT?

WHAT ABOUT HIBERNATION SICKNESS, SIR?

DON'T WORRY, REX, WE WON'T BE FROZEN LONG ENOUGH FOR IT TO TAKE EFFECT.

THE FREEZE CHAMBER IS READY, GENERAL.

ONE QUESTION, MASTER...IF WE'RE ALL FROZEN, WHO'S GONNA FLY US THROUGH THE BLOCKADE?

MY LITTLE BUDDY, ARTOO.

BWEET-DOOOT!

16

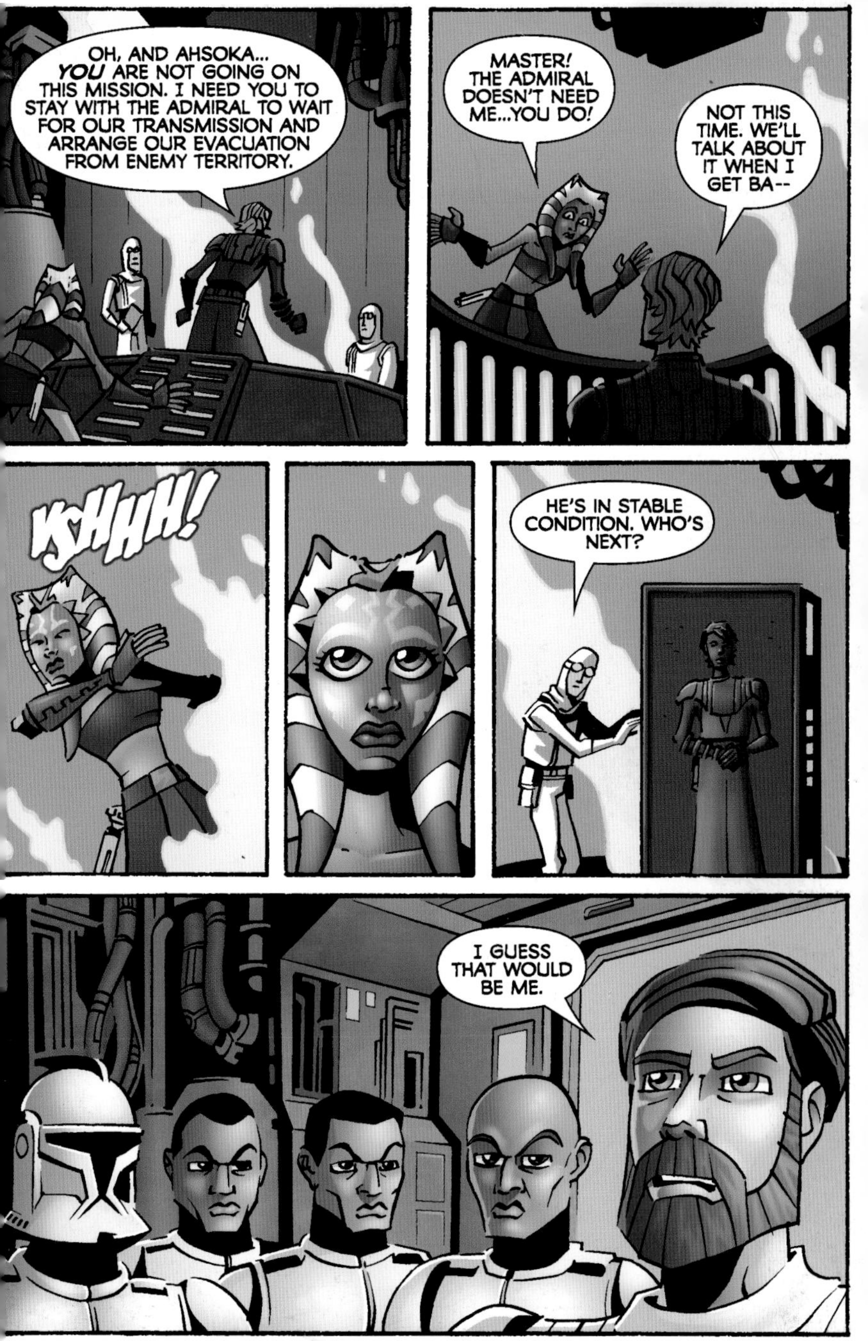
OH, AND AHSOKA... YOU ARE NOT GOING ON THIS MISSION. I NEED YOU TO STAY WITH THE ADMIRAL TO WAIT FOR OUR TRANSMISSION AND ARRANGE OUR EVACUATION FROM ENEMY TERRITORY.
MASTER! THE ADMIRAL DOESN'T NEED ME...YOU DO!
NOT THIS TIME. WE'LL TALK ABOUT IT WHEN I GET BA--
VSHHHH!
HE'S IN STABLE CONDITION. WHO'S NEXT?
I GUESS THAT WOULD BE ME.

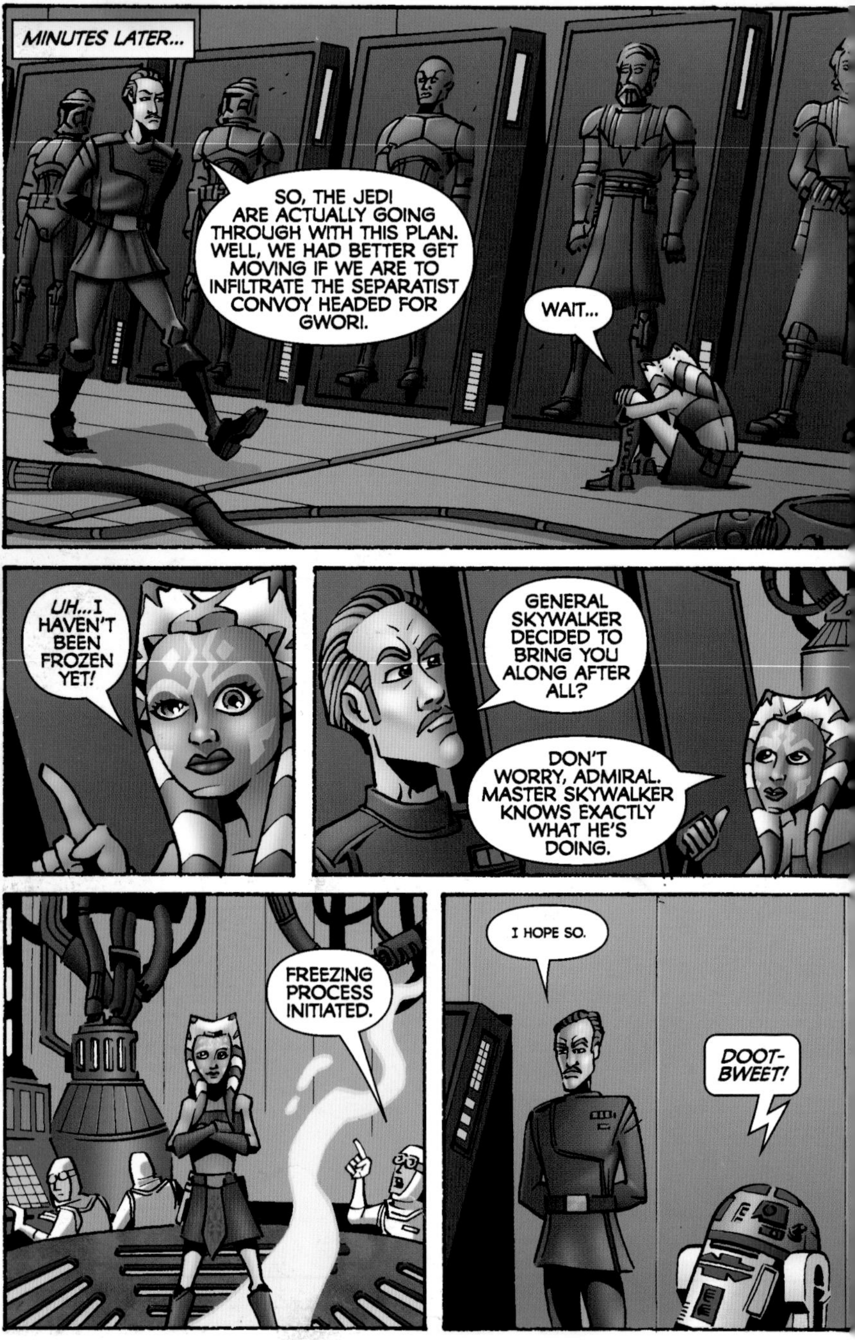
MINUTES LATER...
SO, THE JEDI ARE ACTUALLY GOING THROUGH WITH THIS PLAN. WELL, WE HAD BETTER GET MOVING IF WE ARE TO INFILTRATE THE SEPARATIST CONVOY HEADED FOR GWORI.
WAIT...
UH...I HAVEN'T BEEN FROZEN YET!
GENERAL SKYWALKER DECIDED TO BRING YOU ALONG AFTER ALL?
DON'T WORRY, ADMIRAL. MASTER SKYWALKER KNOWS EXACTLY WHAT HE'S DOING.
FREEZING PROCESS INITIATED.
I HOPE SO.
DOOT-BWEET!

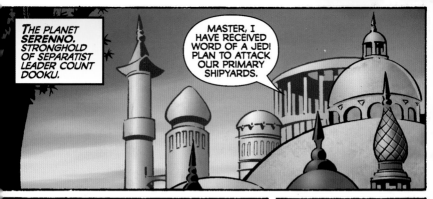

THE PLANET **SERENNO.** STRONGHOLD OF SEPARATIST LEADER COUNT DOOKU.

MASTER, I HAVE RECEIVED WORD OF A JEDI PLAN TO ATTACK OUR PRIMARY SHIPYARDS.

I AM AWARE OF THE PLOT, MY FRIEND, BUT REST ASSURED IT HAS LITTLE CHANCE OF SUCCESS.

CAN WE AFFORD TO TAKE *ANY* CHANCE, MASTER? THE GREATER OUR NAVY, THE LONGER THE WAR WILL GO ON...AND THE MORE JEDI WILL DIE.

WE ARE EARLY IN THIS CONFLICT, LORD TYRANUS. I AM MORE INTERESTED IN LEARNING WHICH OF OUR SEPARATIST PAWNS CAN BE RELIED UPON --

-- AND WHICH JEDI WILL PROVE THEMSELVES AS OUR GREATEST THREATS.

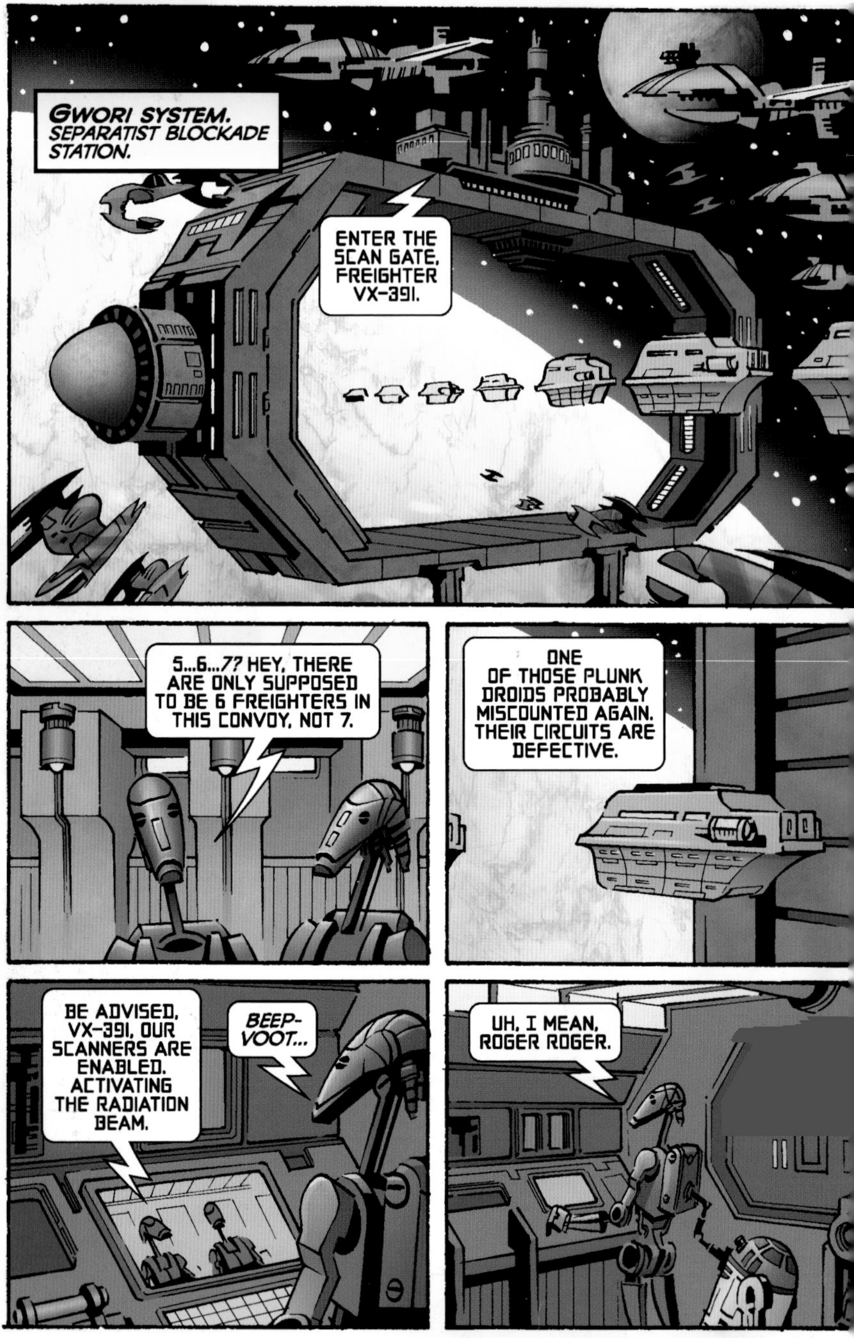
GWORI SYSTEM. SEPARATIST BLOCKADE STATION.
ENTER THE SCAN GATE, FREIGHTER VX-391.
5...6...7? HEY, THERE ARE ONLY SUPPOSED TO BE 6 FREIGHTERS IN THIS CONVOY, NOT 7.
ONE OF THOSE PLUNK DROIDS PROBABLY MISCOUNTED AGAIN. THEIR CIRCUITS ARE DEFECTIVE.
BE ADVISED, VX-391, OUR SCANNERS ARE ENABLED. ACTIVATING THE RADIATION BEAM.
BEEP-VOOT...
UH, I MEAN, ROGER ROGER.

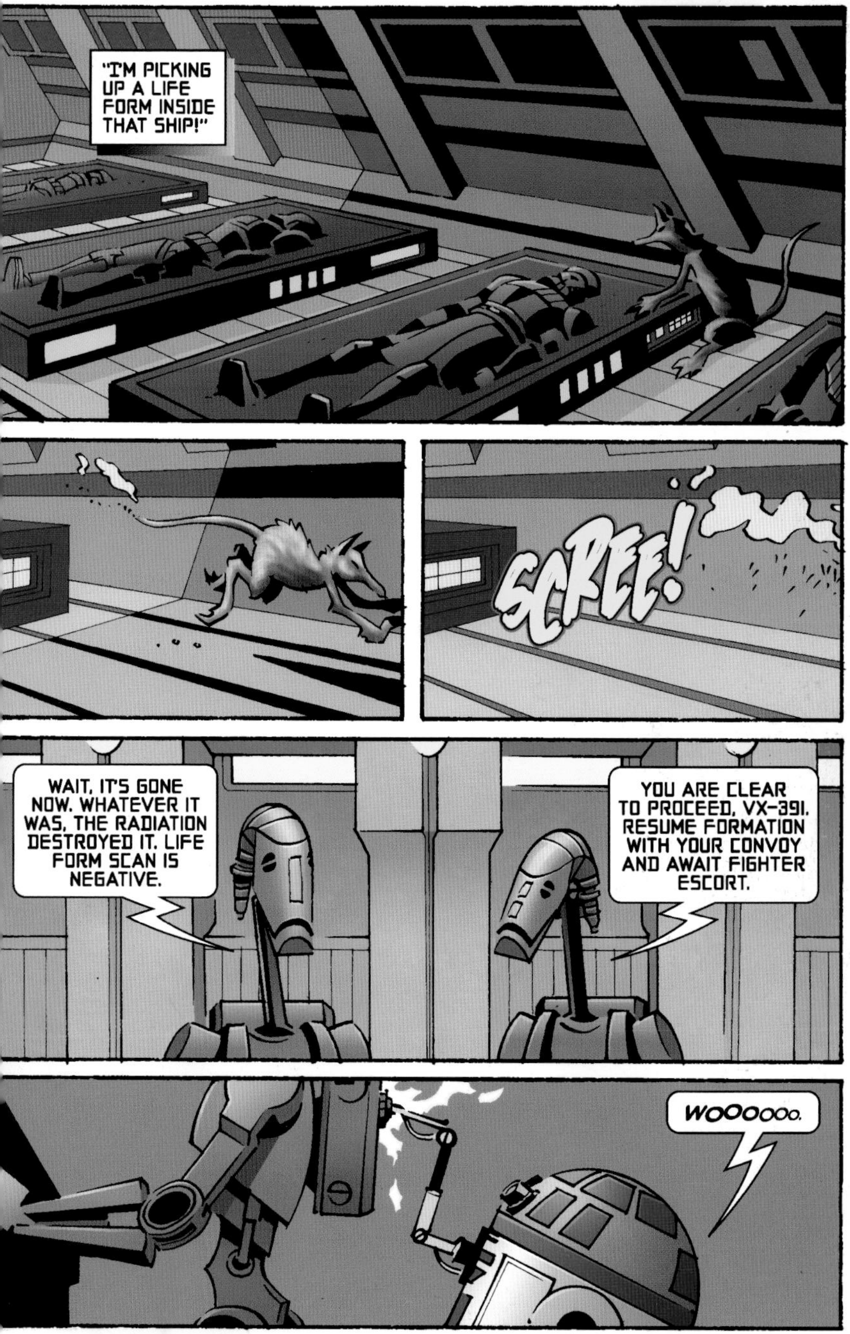
"I'M PICKING UP A LIFE FORM INSIDE THAT SHIP!"
SCREE!
WAIT, IT'S GONE NOW. WHATEVER IT WAS, THE RADIATION DESTROYED IT. LIFE FORM SCAN IS NEGATIVE.
YOU ARE CLEAR TO PROCEED, VX-391. RESUME FORMATION WITH YOUR CONVOY AND AWAIT FIGHTER ESCORT.
WOOOooo.

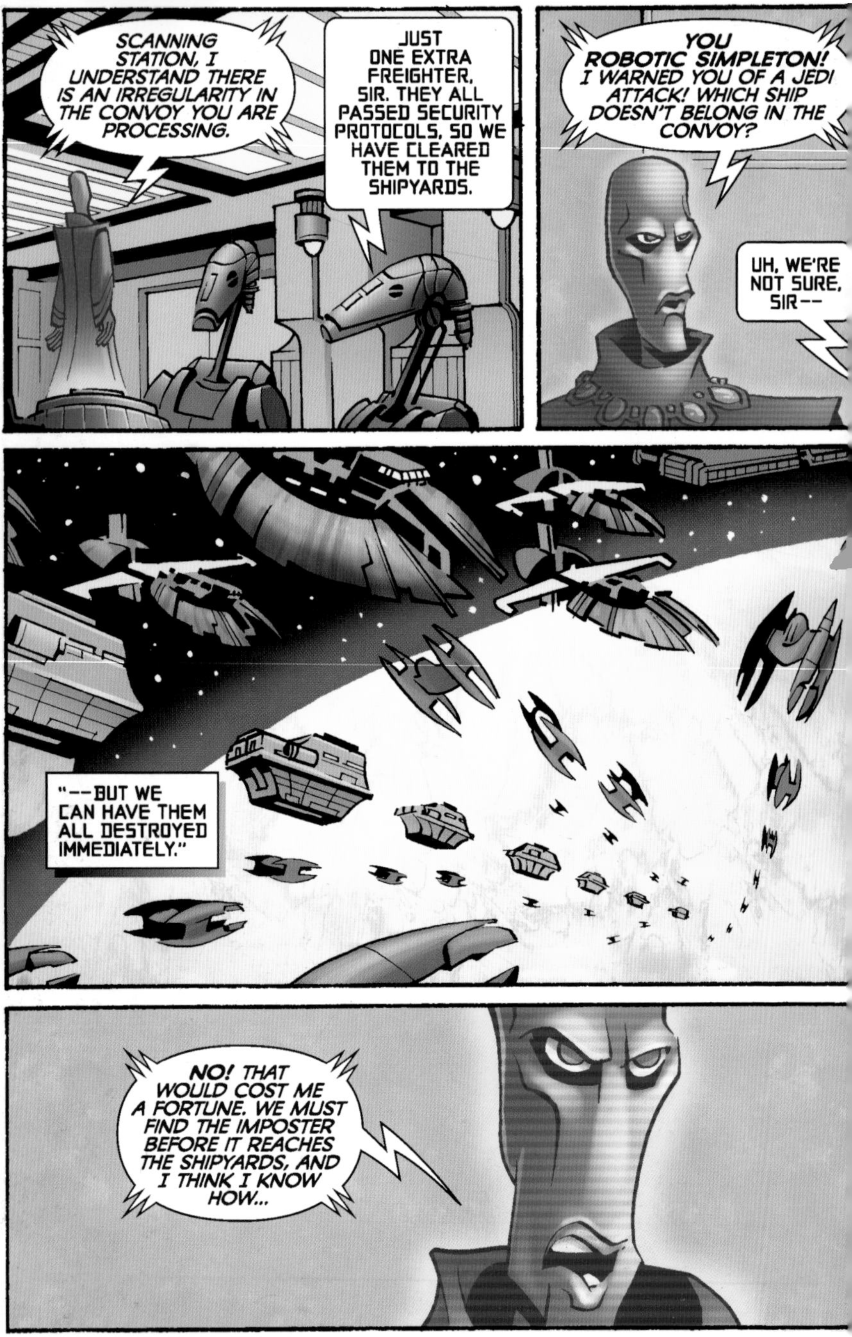
SCANNING STATION, I UNDERSTAND THERE IS AN IRREGULARITY IN THE CONVOY YOU ARE PROCESSING.
JUST ONE EXTRA FREIGHTER, SIR. THEY ALL PASSED SECURITY PROTOCOLS, SO WE HAVE CLEARED THEM TO THE SHIPYARDS.
YOU ROBOTIC SIMPLETON! I WARNED YOU OF A JEDI ATTACK! WHICH SHIP DOESN'T BELONG IN THE CONVOY?
UH, WE'RE NOT SURE, SIR--
"--BUT WE CAN HAVE THEM ALL DESTROYED IMMEDIATELY."
NO! THAT WOULD COST ME A FORTUNE. WE MUST FIND THE IMPOSTER BEFORE IT REACHES THE SHIPYARDS, AND I THINK I KNOW HOW...

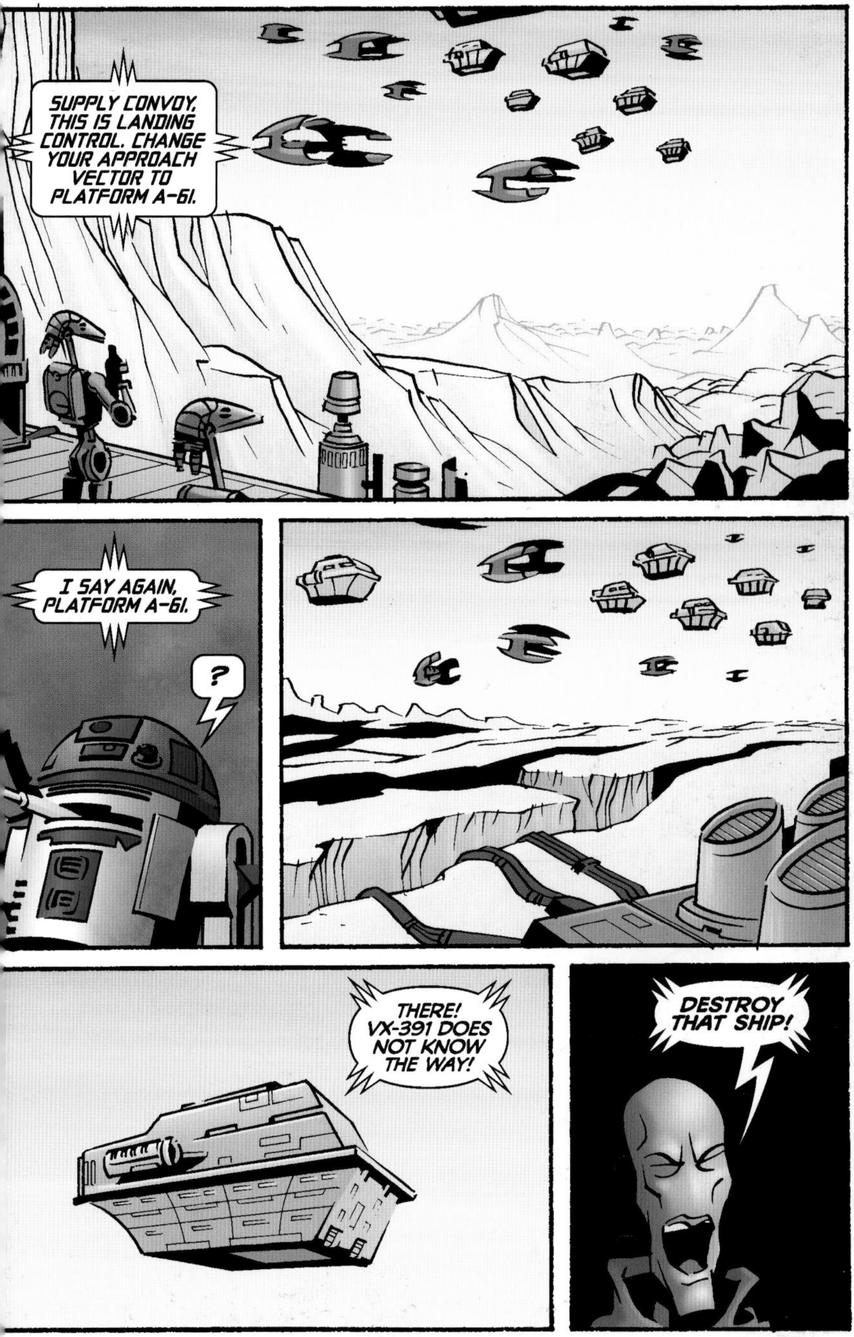
SUPPLY CONVOY, THIS IS LANDING CONTROL. CHANGE YOUR APPROACH VECTOR TO PLATFORM A-61.
I SAY AGAIN, PLATFORM A-61.
?
THERE! VX-391 DOES NOT KNOW THE WAY!
DESTROY THAT SHIP!

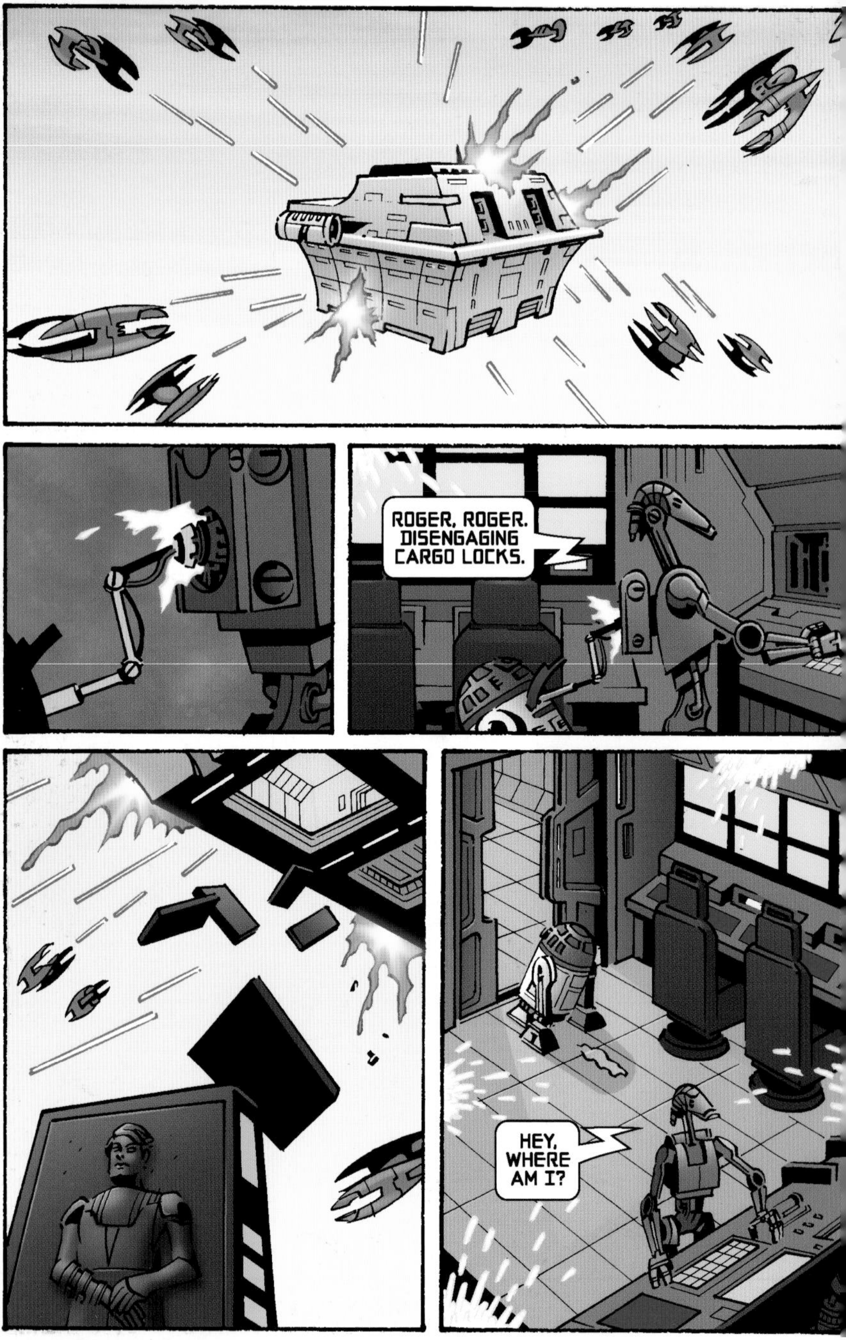
ROGER, ROGER. DISENGAGING CARGO LOCKS.
HEY, WHERE AM I?

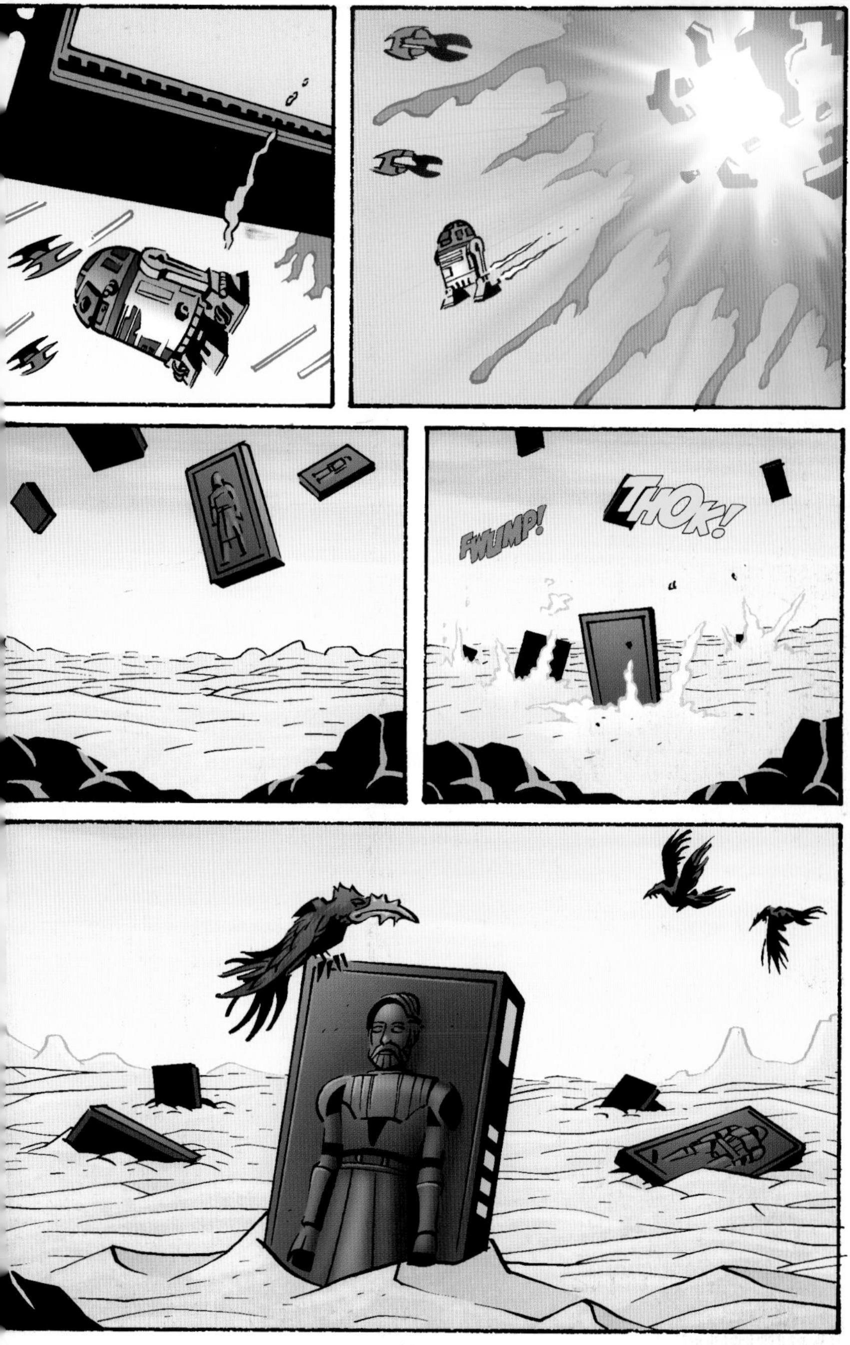
FWUMP!
THOK!

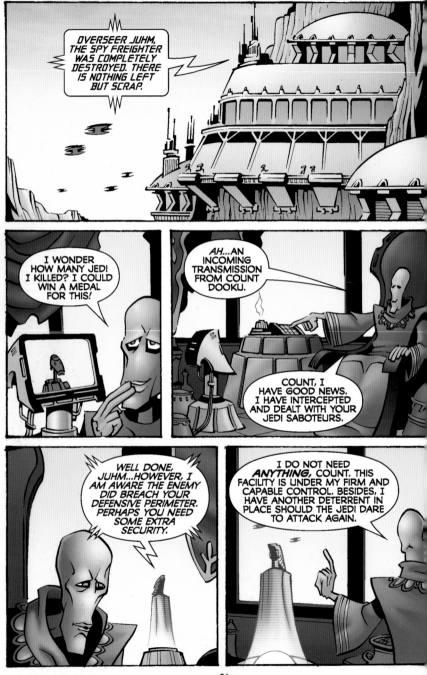

OVERSEER JUHM, THE SPY FREIGHTER WAS COMPLETELY DESTROYED. THERE IS NOTHING LEFT BUT SCRAP.

I WONDER HOW MANY JEDI I KILLED? I COULD WIN A MEDAL FOR THIS!

AH...AN INCOMING TRANSMISSION FROM COUNT DOOKU.

COUNT, I HAVE GOOD NEWS. I HAVE INTERCEPTED AND DEALT WITH YOUR JEDI SABOTEURS.

WELL DONE, JUHM...HOWEVER, I AM AWARE THE ENEMY DID BREACH YOUR DEFENSIVE PERIMETER. PERHAPS YOU NEED SOME EXTRA SECURITY.

I DO NOT NEED *ANYTHING*, COUNT. THIS FACILITY IS UNDER MY FIRM AND CAPABLE CONTROL. BESIDES, I HAVE ANOTHER DETERRENT IN PLACE SHOULD THE JEDI DARE TO ATTACK AGAIN.

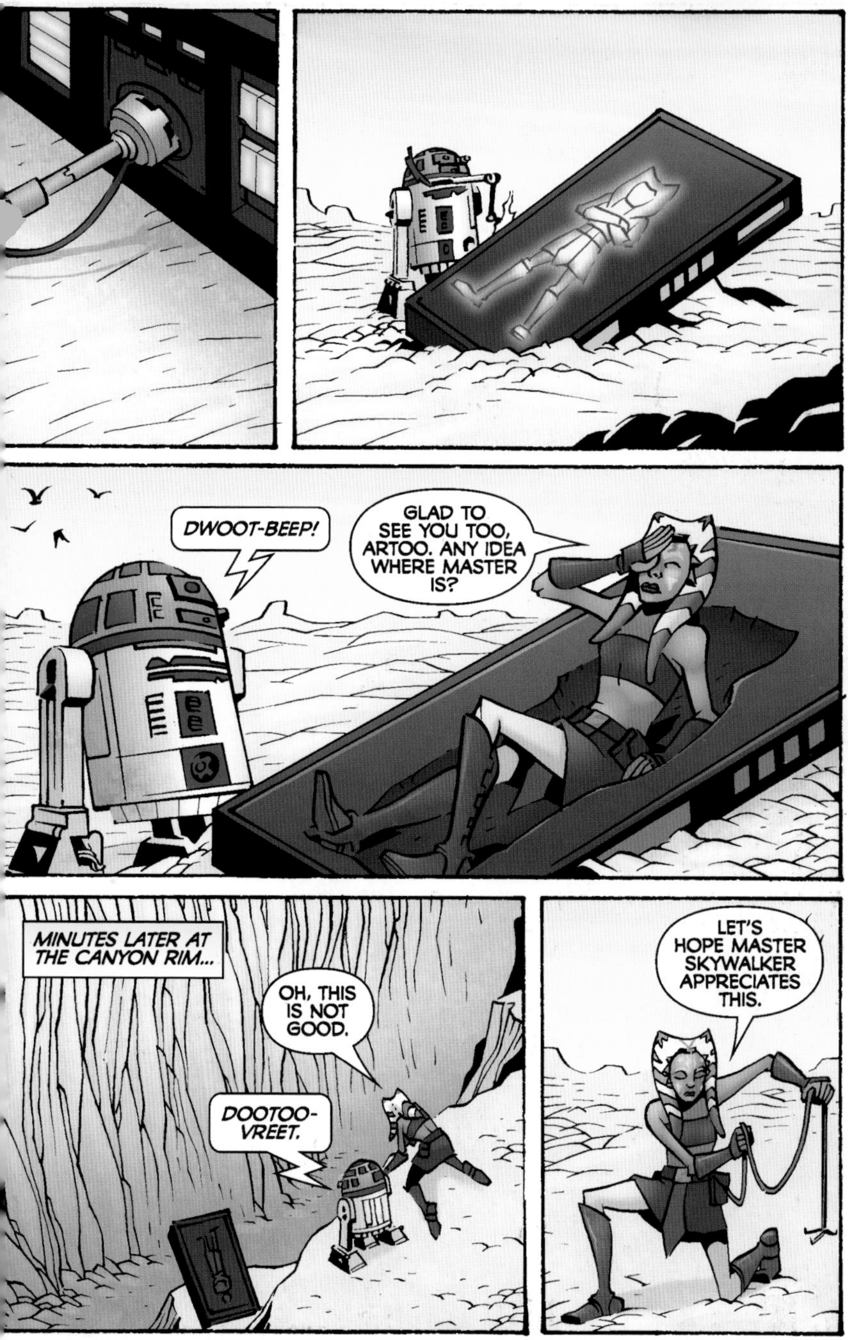
DWOOT-BEEP!
GLAD TO SEE YOU TOO, ARTOO. ANY IDEA WHERE MASTER IS?
MINUTES LATER AT THE CANYON RIM...
OH, THIS IS NOT GOOD.
DOOTOO-VREET.
LET'S HOPE MASTER SKYWALKER APPRECIATES THIS.

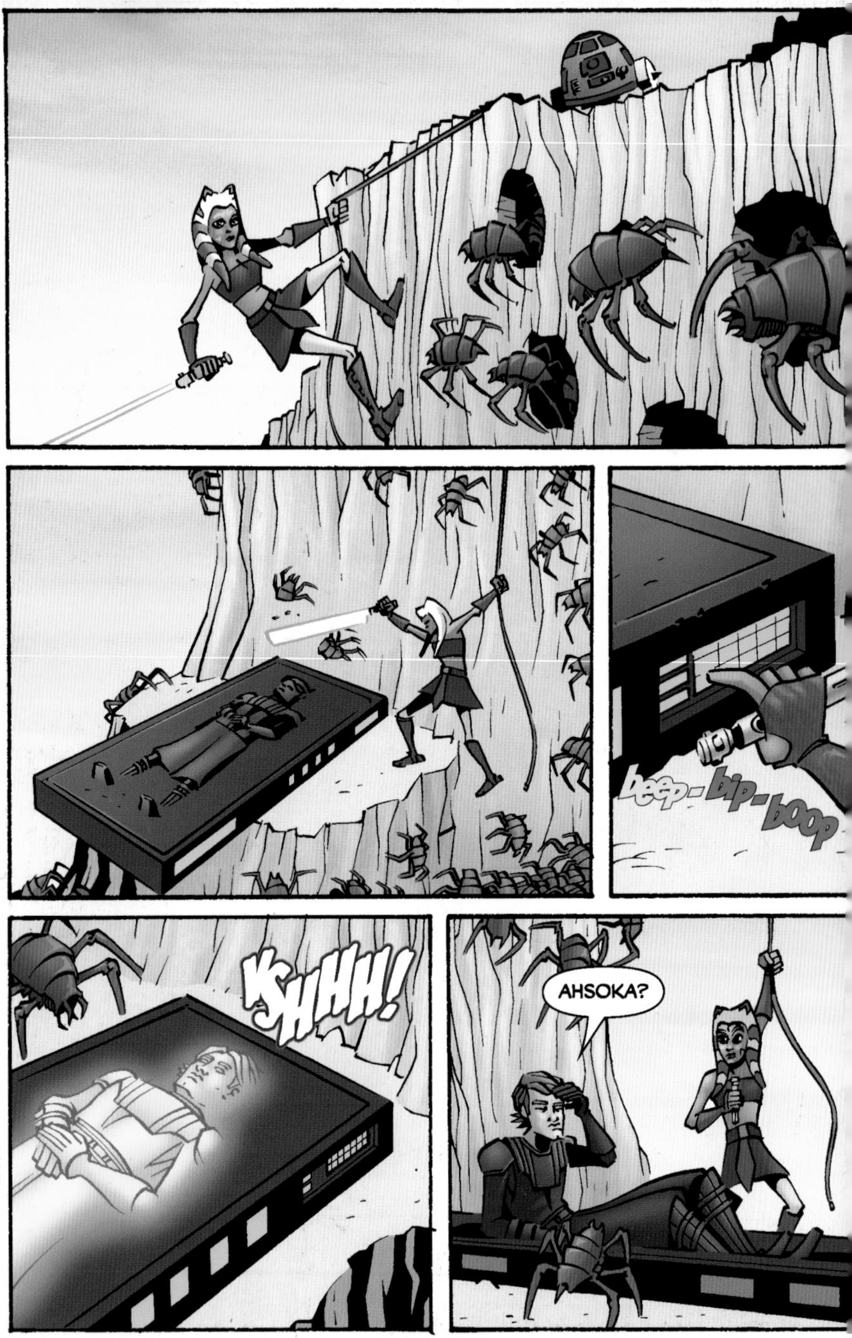
beep-bip-boop
VSHHH!
AHSOKA?

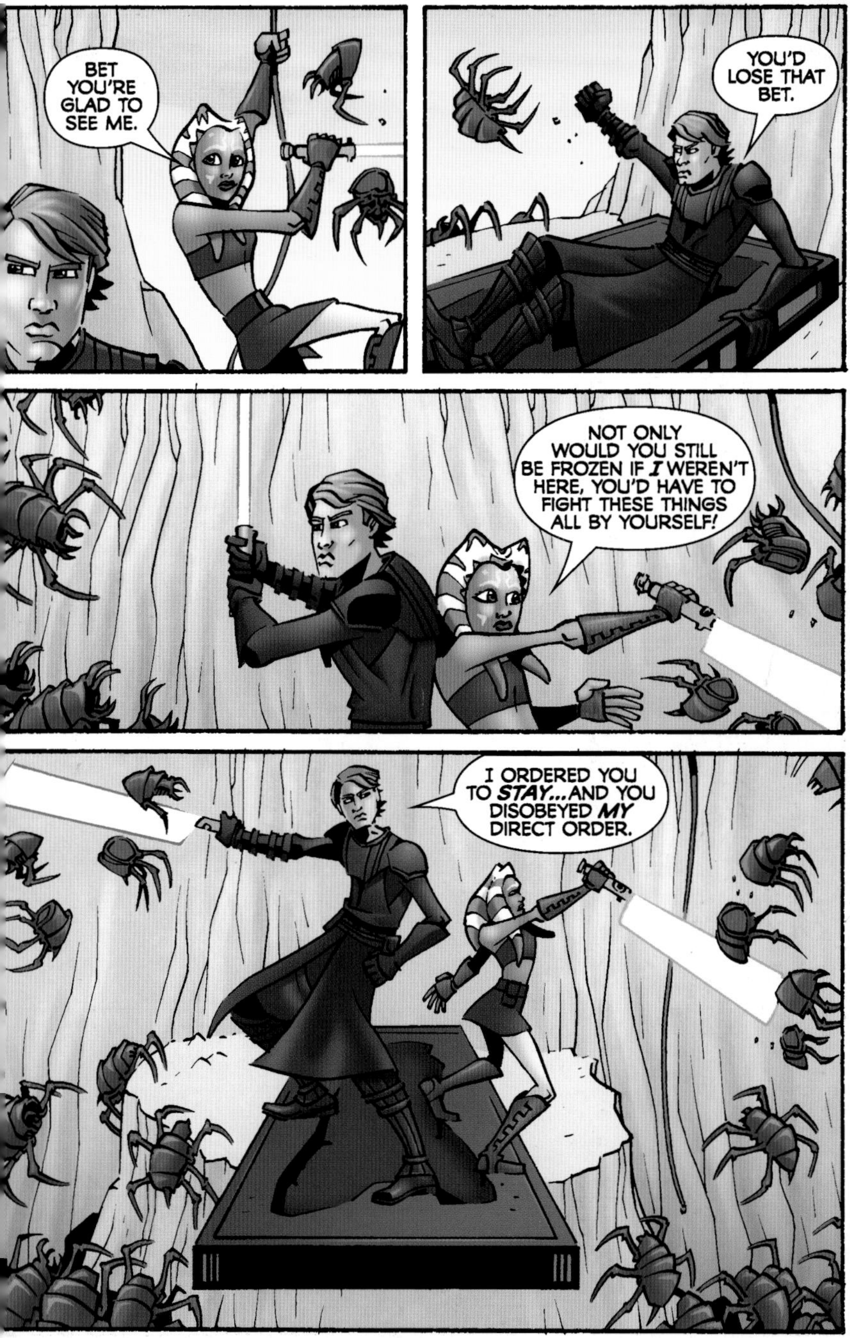
BET YOU'RE GLAD TO SEE ME.
YOU'D LOSE THAT BET.
NOT ONLY WOULD YOU STILL BE FROZEN IF *I* WEREN'T HERE, YOU'D HAVE TO FIGHT THESE THINGS ALL BY YOURSELF!
I ORDERED YOU TO *STAY*...AND YOU DISOBEYED *MY* DIRECT ORDER.

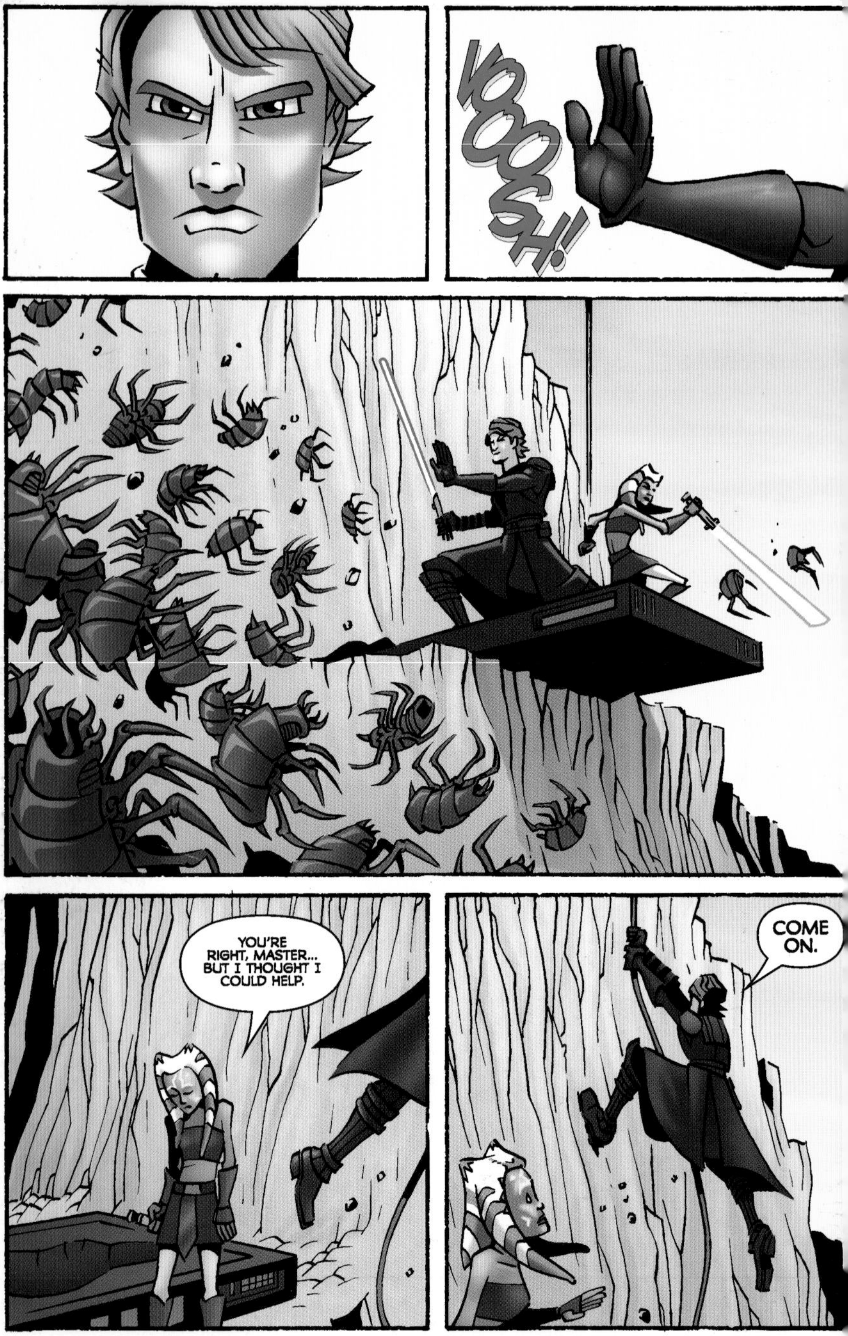
VOOOOSH!
YOU'RE RIGHT, MASTER... BUT I THOUGHT I COULD HELP.
COME ON.

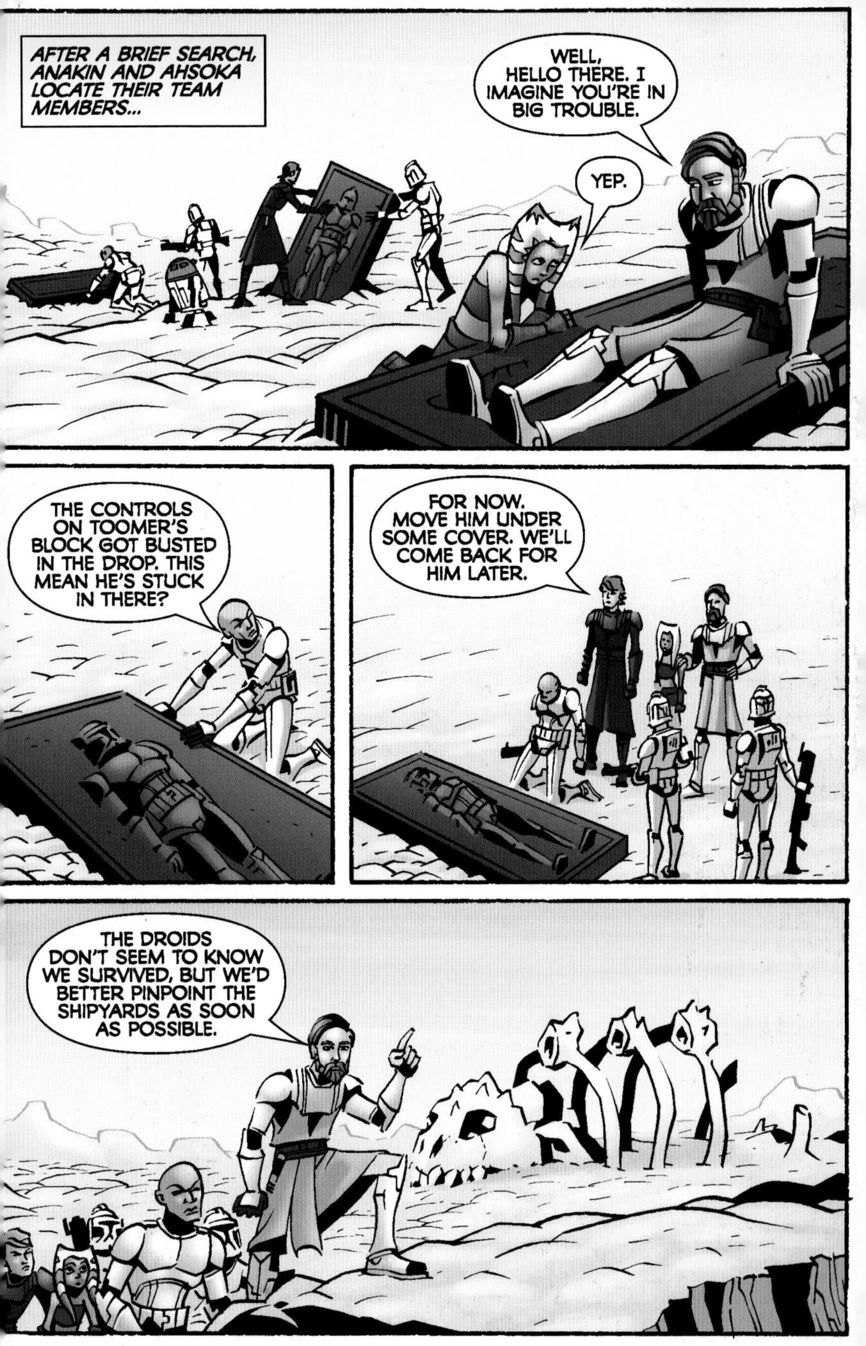
AFTER A BRIEF SEARCH, ANAKIN AND AHSOKA LOCATE THEIR TEAM MEMBERS...
WELL, HELLO THERE. I IMAGINE YOU'RE IN BIG TROUBLE.
YEP.
THE CONTROLS ON TOOMER'S BLOCK GOT BUSTED IN THE DROP. THIS MEAN HE'S STUCK IN THERE?
FOR NOW. MOVE HIM UNDER SOME COVER. WE'LL COME BACK FOR HIM LATER.
THE DROIDS DON'T SEEM TO KNOW WE SURVIVED, BUT WE'D BETTER PINPOINT THE SHIPYARDS AS SOON AS POSSIBLE.

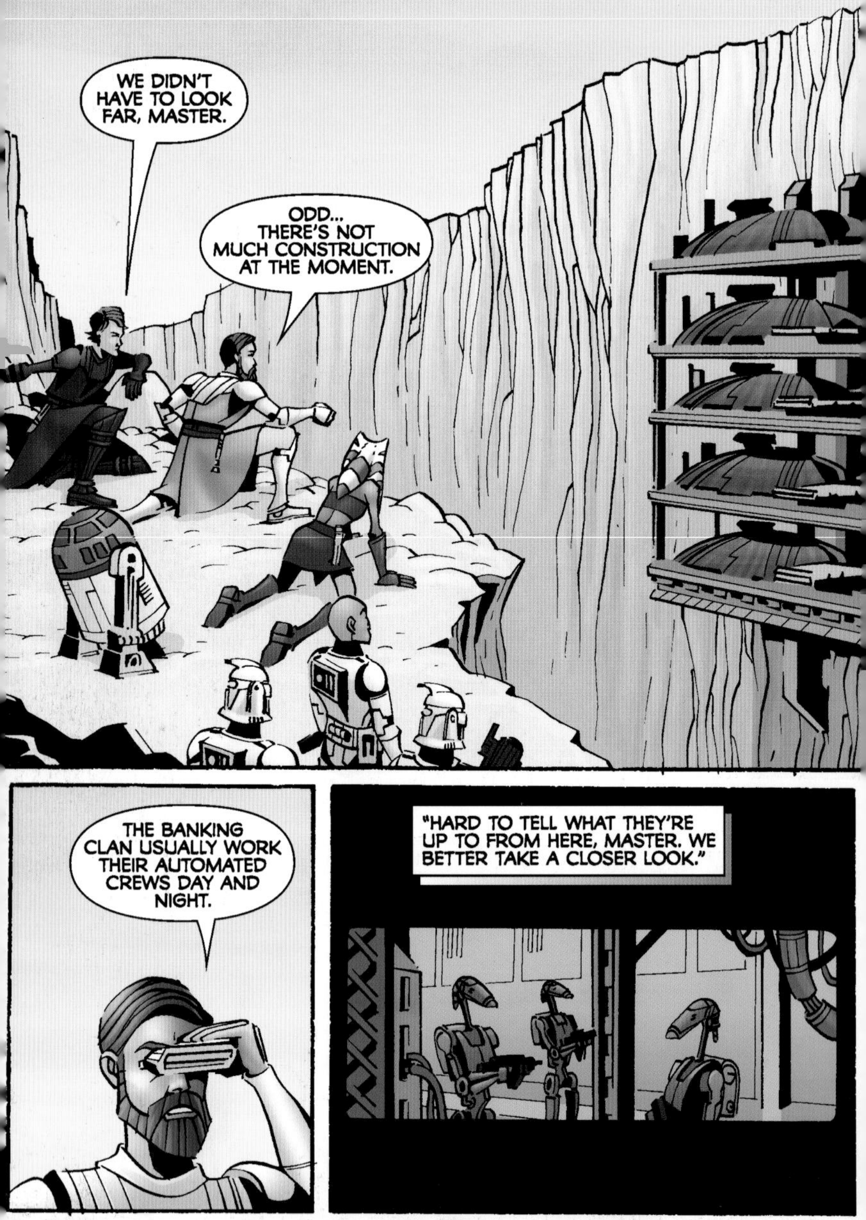
WE DIDN'T HAVE TO LOOK FAR, MASTER.
ODD... THERE'S NOT MUCH CONSTRUCTION AT THE MOMENT.
THE BANKING CLAN USUALLY WORK THEIR AUTOMATED CREWS DAY AND NIGHT.
"HARD TO TELL WHAT THEY'RE UP TO FROM HERE, MASTER. WE BETTER TAKE A CLOSER LOOK."

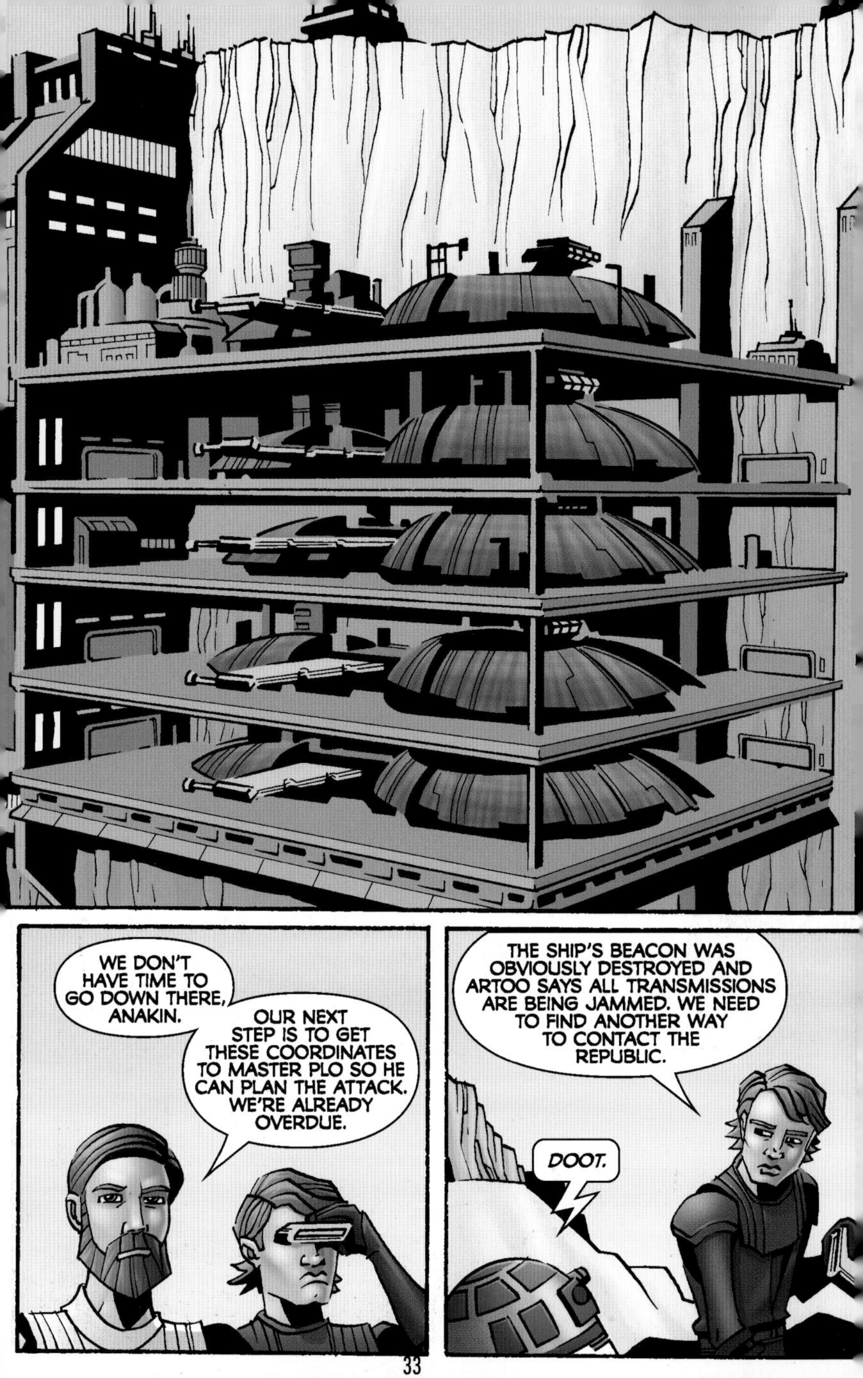
WE DON'T HAVE TIME TO GO DOWN THERE, ANAKIN.
OUR NEXT STEP IS TO GET THESE COORDINATES TO MASTER PLO SO HE CAN PLAN THE ATTACK. WE'RE ALREADY OVERDUE.
THE SHIP'S BEACON WAS OBVIOUSLY DESTROYED AND ARTOO SAYS ALL TRANSMISSIONS ARE BEING JAMMED. WE NEED TO FIND ANOTHER WAY TO CONTACT THE REPUBLIC.
DOOT.

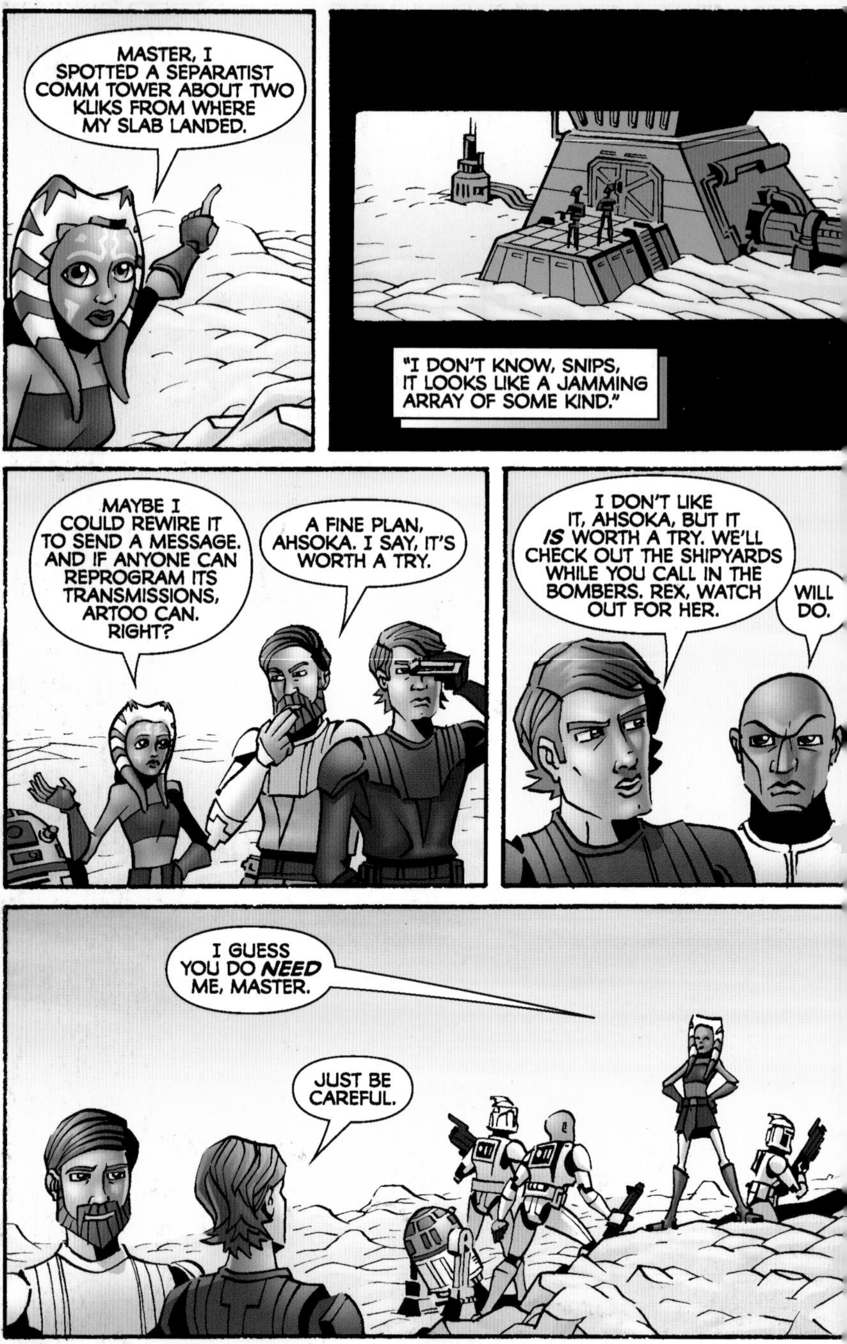
MASTER, I SPOTTED A SEPARATIST COMM TOWER ABOUT TWO KLIKS FROM WHERE MY SLAB LANDED.
"I DON'T KNOW, SNIPS, IT LOOKS LIKE A JAMMING ARRAY OF SOME KIND."
MAYBE I COULD REWIRE IT TO SEND A MESSAGE. AND IF ANYONE CAN REPROGRAM ITS TRANSMISSIONS, ARTOO CAN. RIGHT?
A FINE PLAN, AHSOKA. I SAY, IT'S WORTH A TRY.
I DON'T LIKE IT, AHSOKA, BUT IT *IS* WORTH A TRY. WE'LL CHECK OUT THE SHIPYARDS WHILE YOU CALL IN THE BOMBERS. REX, WATCH OUT FOR HER.
WILL DO.
I GUESS YOU DO ***NEED*** ME, MASTER.
JUST BE CAREFUL.

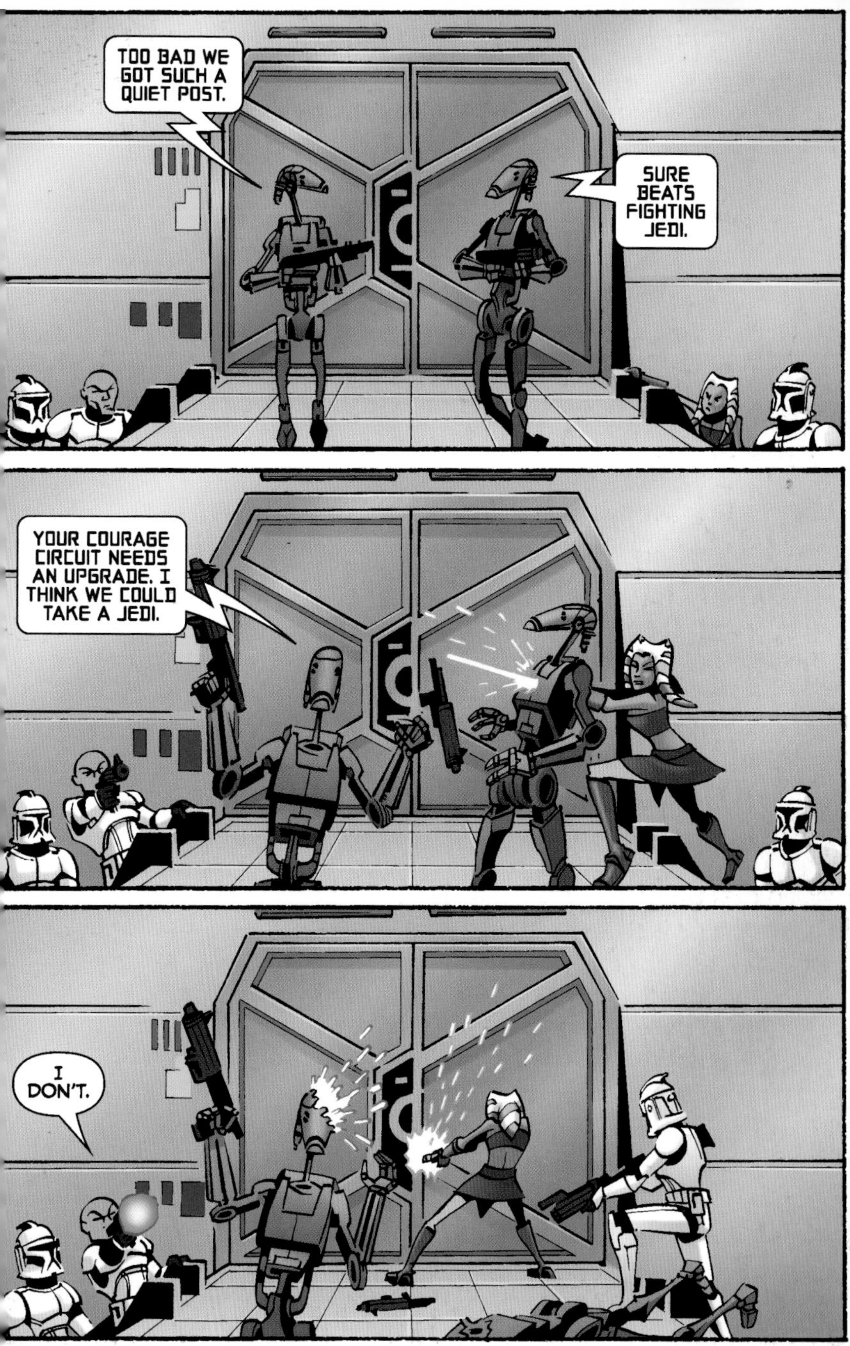

TOO BAD WE GOT SUCH A QUIET POST.
SURE BEATS FIGHTING JEDI.
YOUR COURAGE CIRCUIT NEEDS AN UPGRADE. I THINK WE COULD TAKE A JEDI.
I DON'T.

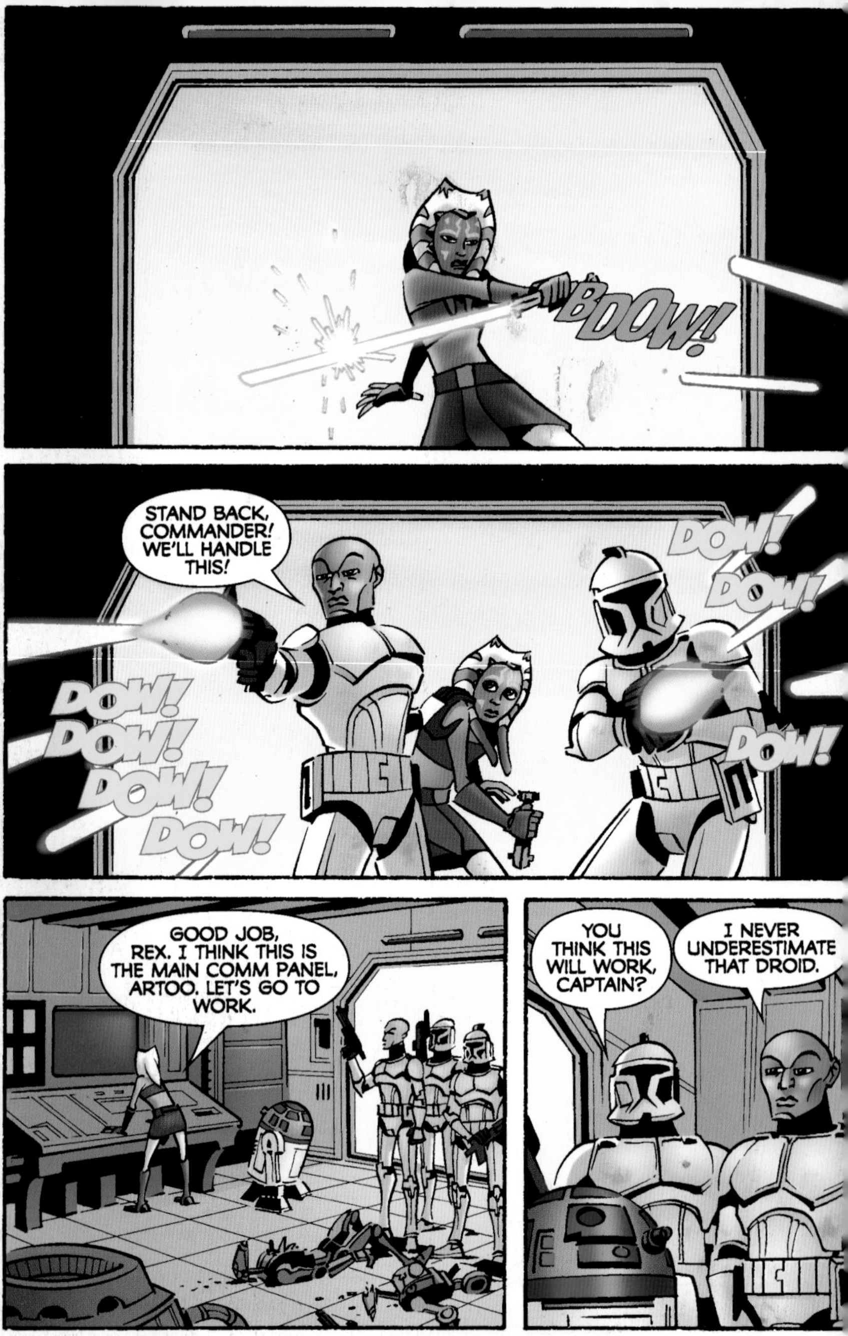
BDOW!
STAND BACK, COMMANDER! WE'LL HANDLE THIS!
DOW!
DOW!
DOW!
DOW!
DOW!
DOW!
DOW!
GOOD JOB, REX. I THINK THIS IS THE MAIN COMM PANEL, ARTOO. LET'S GO TO WORK.
YOU THINK THIS WILL WORK, CAPTAIN?
I NEVER UNDERESTIMATE THAT DROID.

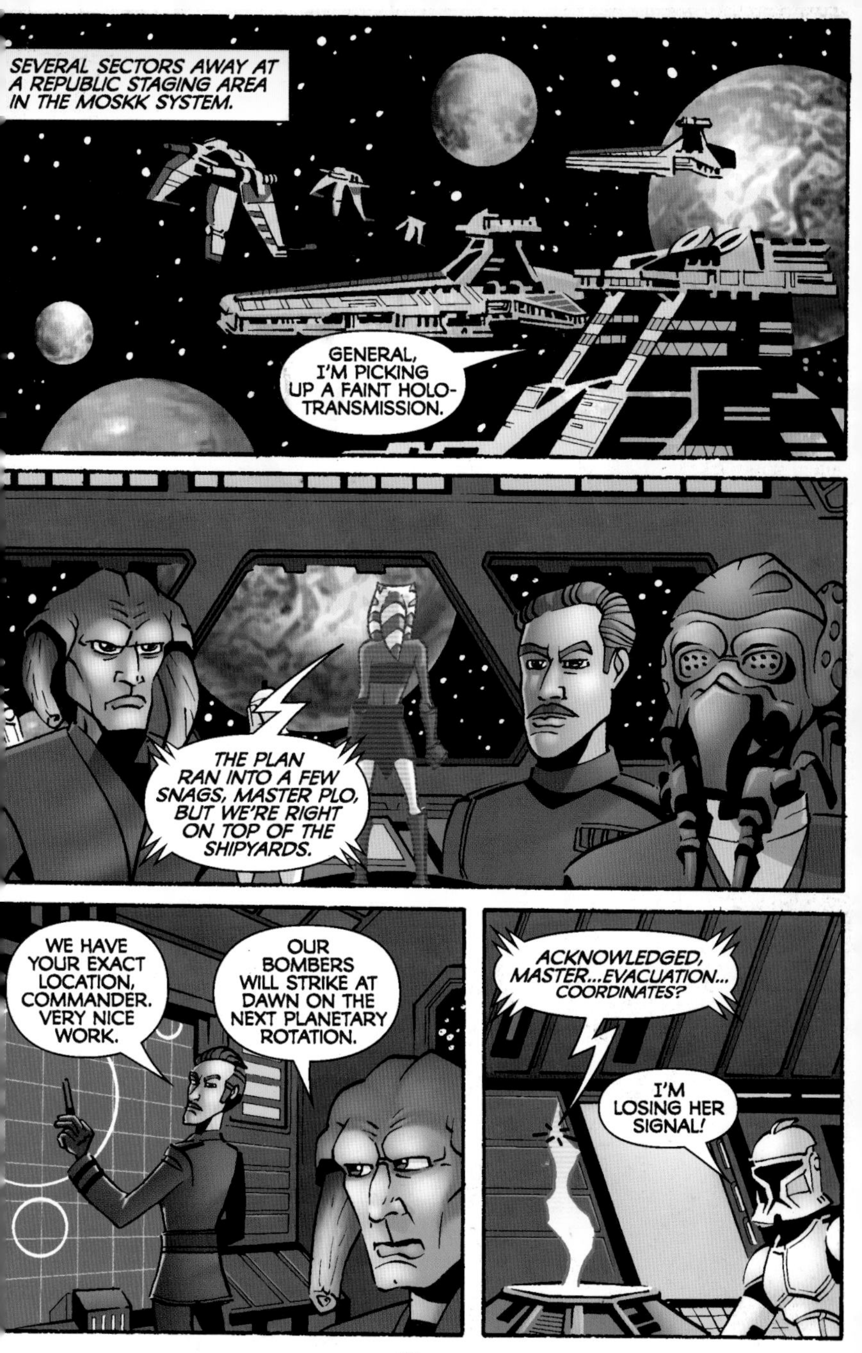
SEVERAL SECTORS AWAY AT A REPUBLIC STAGING AREA IN THE MOSKK SYSTEM.
GENERAL, I'M PICKING UP A FAINT HOLO-TRANSMISSION.
THE PLAN RAN INTO A FEW SNAGS, MASTER PLO, BUT WE'RE RIGHT ON TOP OF THE SHIPYARDS.
WE HAVE YOUR EXACT LOCATION, COMMANDER. VERY NICE WORK.
OUR BOMBERS WILL STRIKE AT DAWN ON THE NEXT PLANETARY ROTATION.
ACKNOWLEDGED, MASTER...EVACUATION... COORDINATES?
I'M LOSING HER SIGNAL!

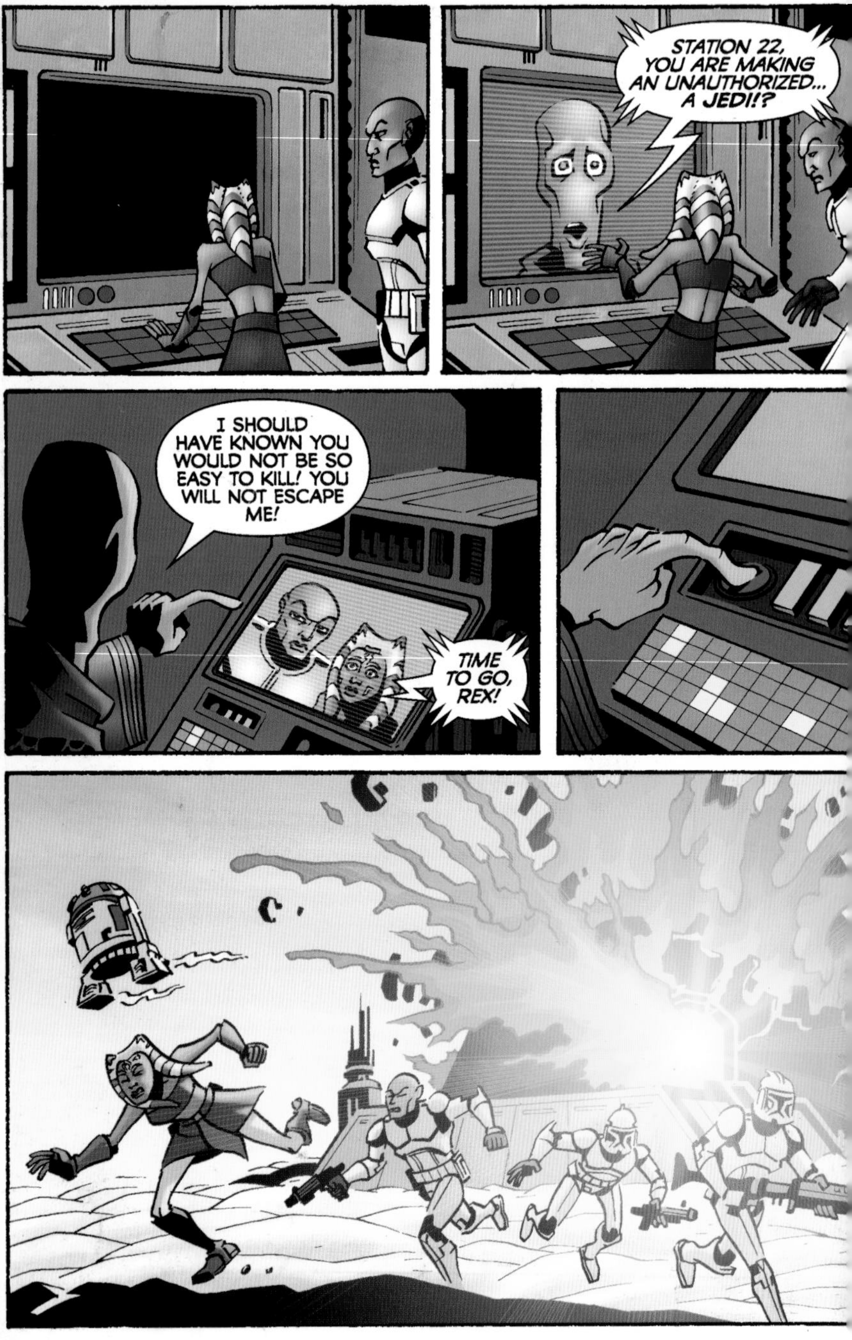
STATION 22, YOU ARE MAKING AN UNAUTHORIZED... A JEDI!?
I SHOULD HAVE KNOWN YOU WOULD NOT BE SO EASY TO KILL! YOU WILL NOT ESCAPE ME!
TIME TO GO, REX!

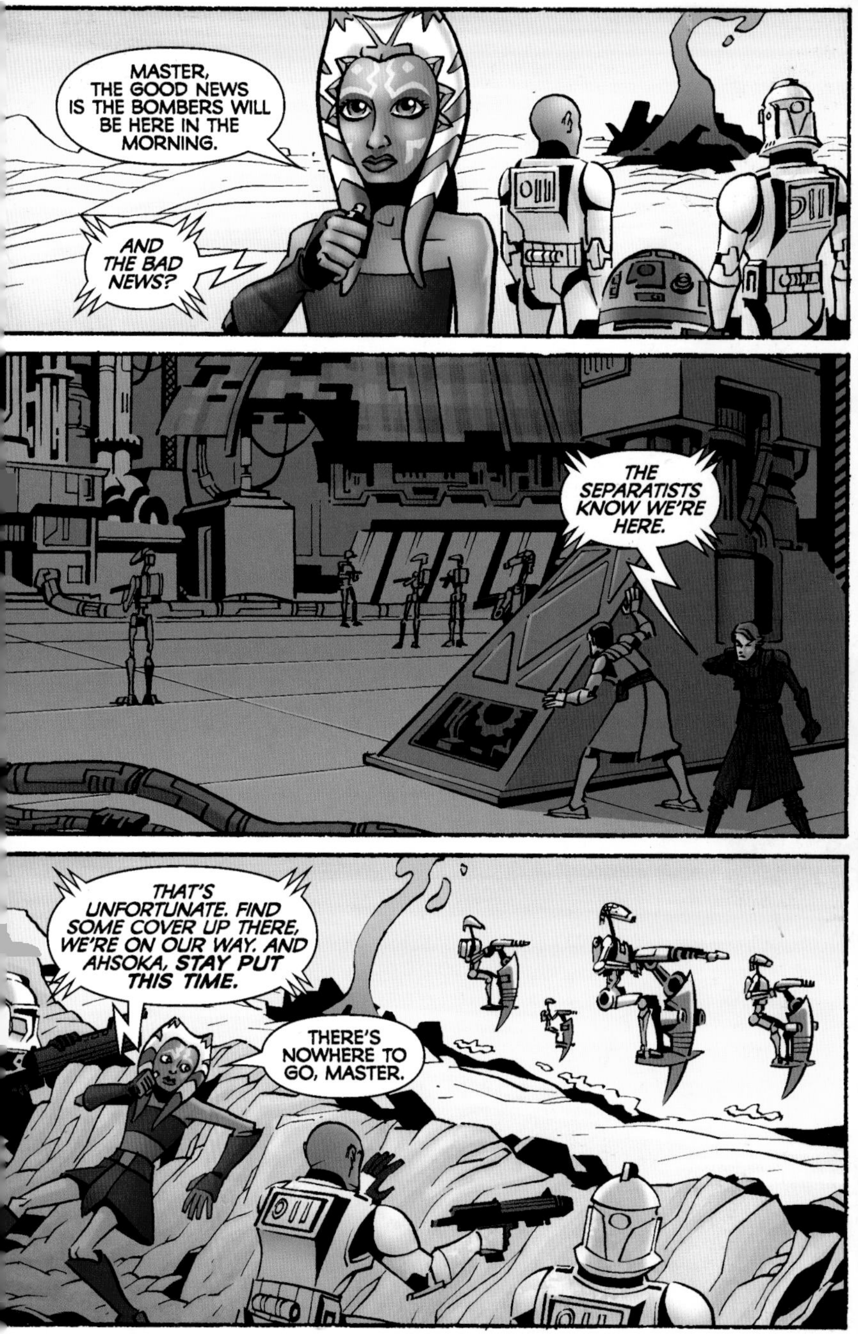

MASTER, THE GOOD NEWS IS THE BOMBERS WILL BE HERE IN THE MORNING.
AND THE BAD NEWS?
THE SEPARATISTS KNOW WE'RE HERE.
THAT'S UNFORTUNATE. FIND SOME COVER UP THERE, WE'RE ON OUR WAY. AND AHSOKA, STAY PUT THIS TIME.
THERE'S NOWHERE TO GO, MASTER.

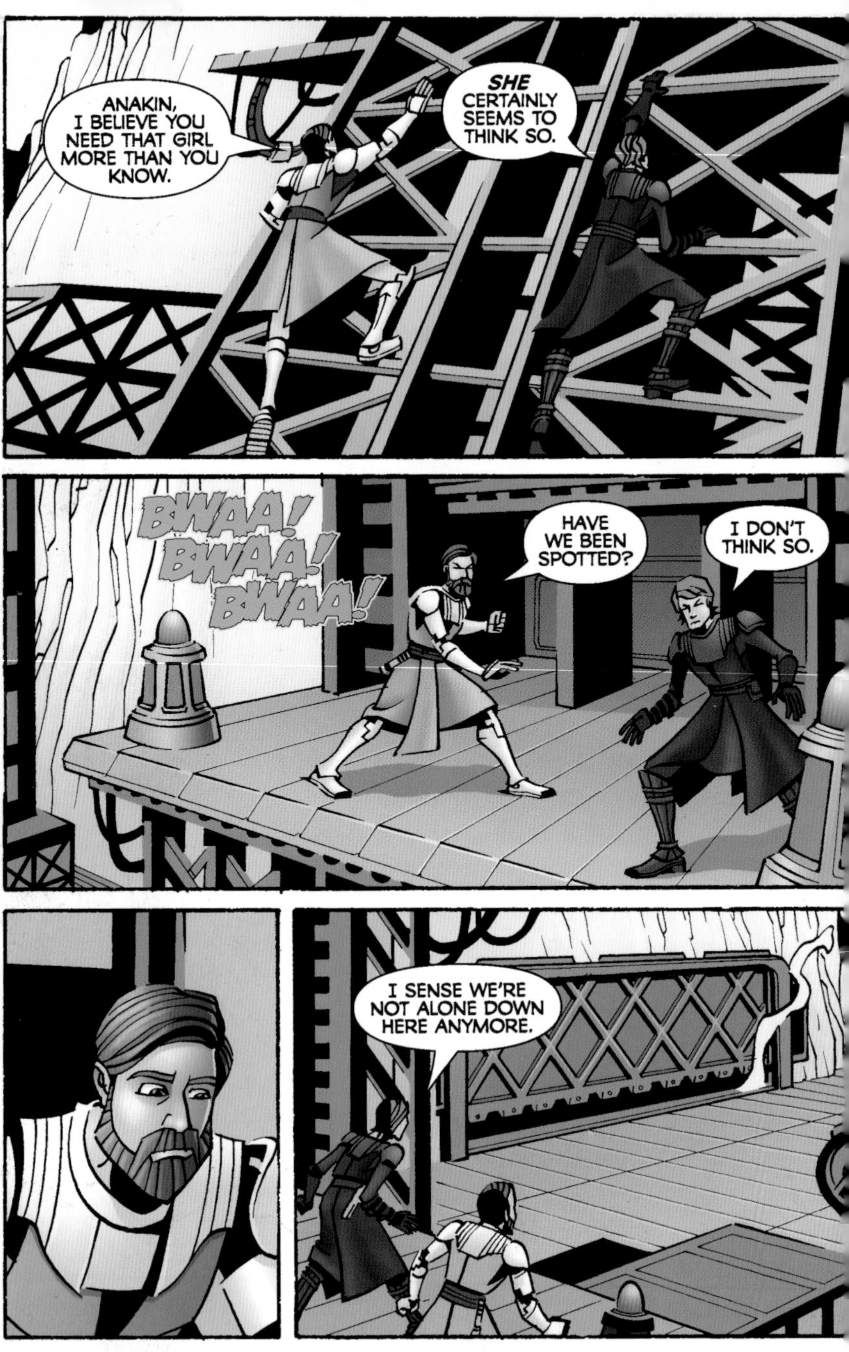
ANAKIN, I BELIEVE YOU NEED THAT GIRL MORE THAN YOU KNOW.
SHE CERTAINLY SEEMS TO THINK SO.
BWAA! BWAA! BWAA!
HAVE WE BEEN SPOTTED?
I DON'T THINK SO.
I SENSE WE'RE NOT ALONE DOWN HERE ANYMORE.

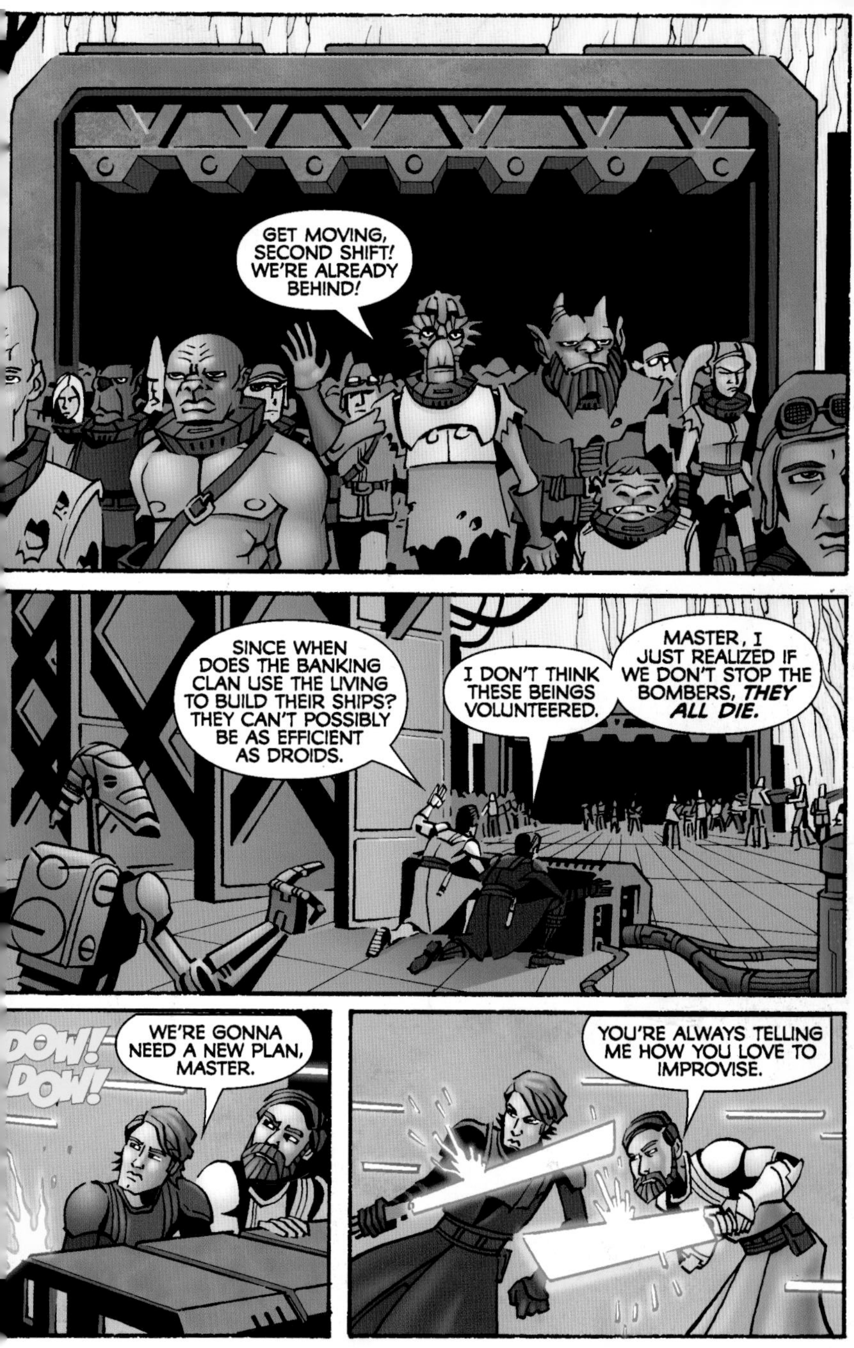
GET MOVING, SECOND SHIFT! WE'RE ALREADY BEHIND!
SINCE WHEN DOES THE BANKING CLAN USE THE LIVING TO BUILD THEIR SHIPS? THEY CAN'T POSSIBLY BE AS EFFICIENT AS DROIDS.
I DON'T THINK THESE BEINGS VOLUNTEERED.
MASTER, I JUST REALIZED IF WE DON'T STOP THE BOMBERS, *THEY ALL DIE.*
DOW! DOW!
WE'RE GONNA NEED A NEW PLAN, MASTER.
YOU'RE ALWAYS TELLING ME HOW YOU LOVE TO IMPROVISE.

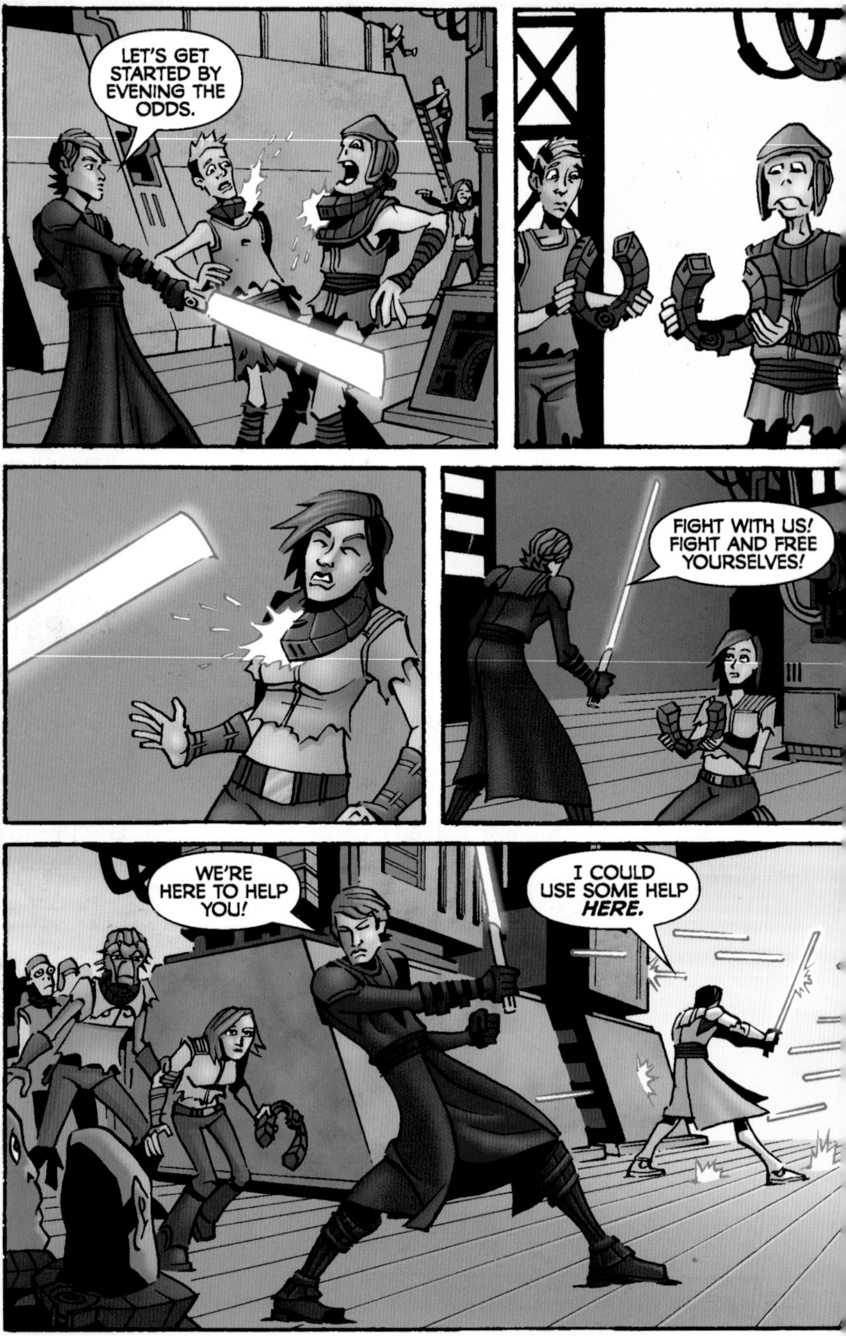
LET'S GET STARTED BY EVENING THE ODDS.
FIGHT WITH US! FIGHT AND FREE YOURSELVES!
WE'RE HERE TO HELP YOU!
I COULD USE SOME HELP *HERE.*

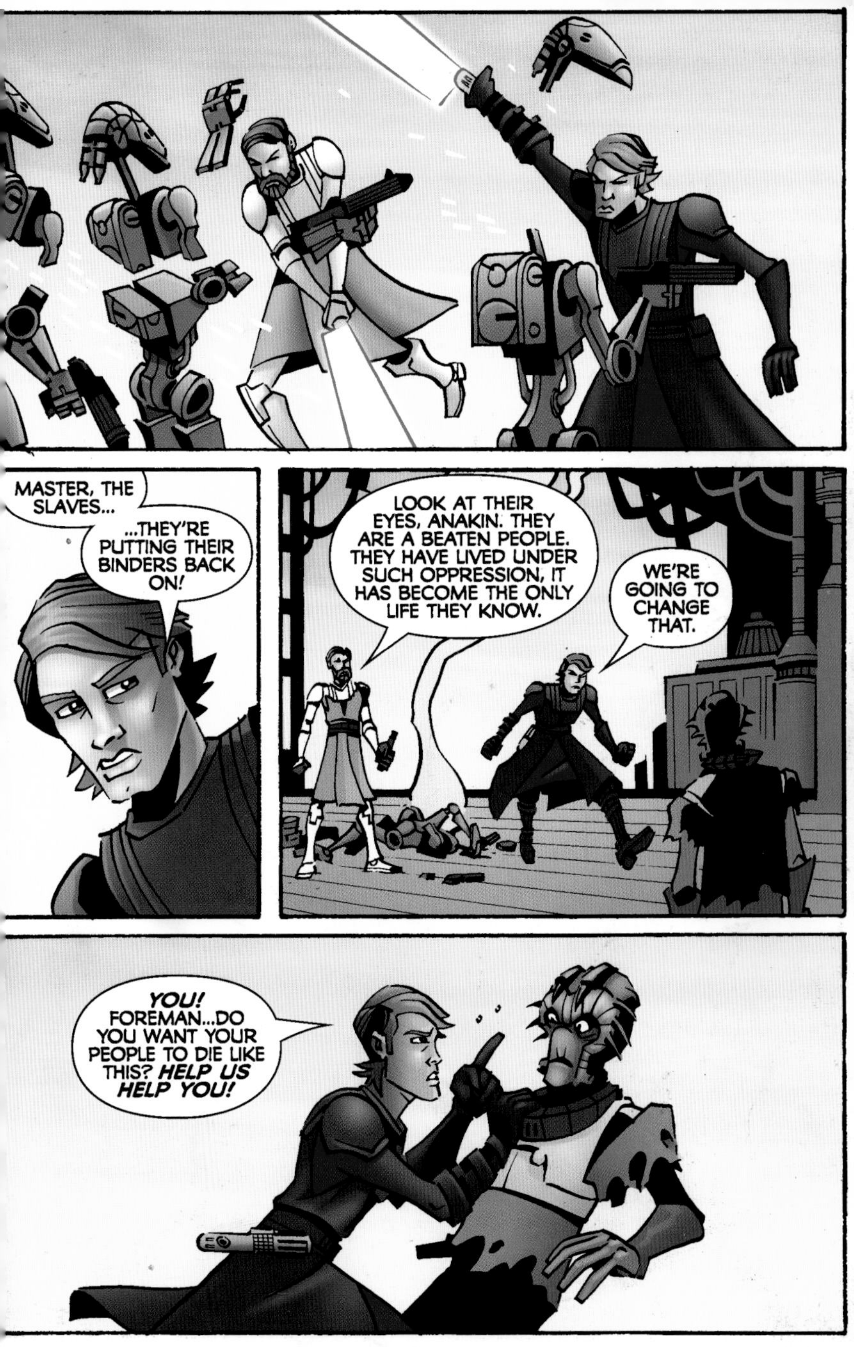
MASTER, THE SLAVES...
...THEY'RE PUTTING THEIR BINDERS BACK ON!
LOOK AT THEIR EYES, ANAKIN. THEY ARE A BEATEN PEOPLE. THEY HAVE LIVED UNDER SUCH OPPRESSION, IT HAS BECOME THE ONLY LIFE THEY KNOW.
WE'RE GOING TO CHANGE THAT.
YOU! FOREMAN...DO YOU WANT YOUR PEOPLE TO DIE LIKE THIS? *HELP US HELP YOU!*

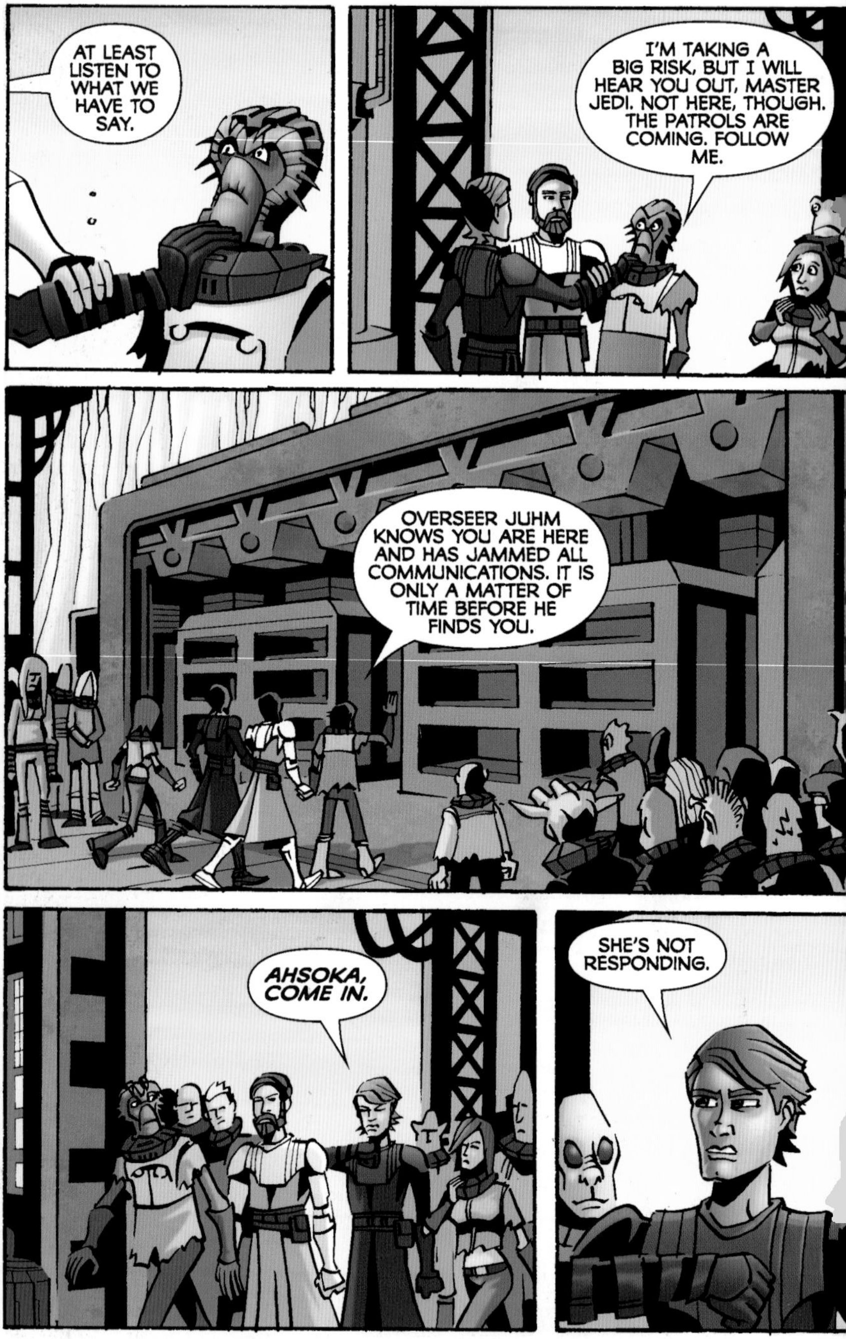
AT LEAST LISTEN TO WHAT WE HAVE TO SAY.
I'M TAKING A BIG RISK, BUT I WILL HEAR YOU OUT, MASTER JEDI. NOT HERE, THOUGH. THE PATROLS ARE COMING. FOLLOW ME.
OVERSEER JUHM KNOWS YOU ARE HERE AND HAS JAMMED ALL COMMUNICATIONS. IT IS ONLY A MATTER OF TIME BEFORE HE FINDS YOU.
AHSOKA, COME IN.
SHE'S NOT RESPONDING.

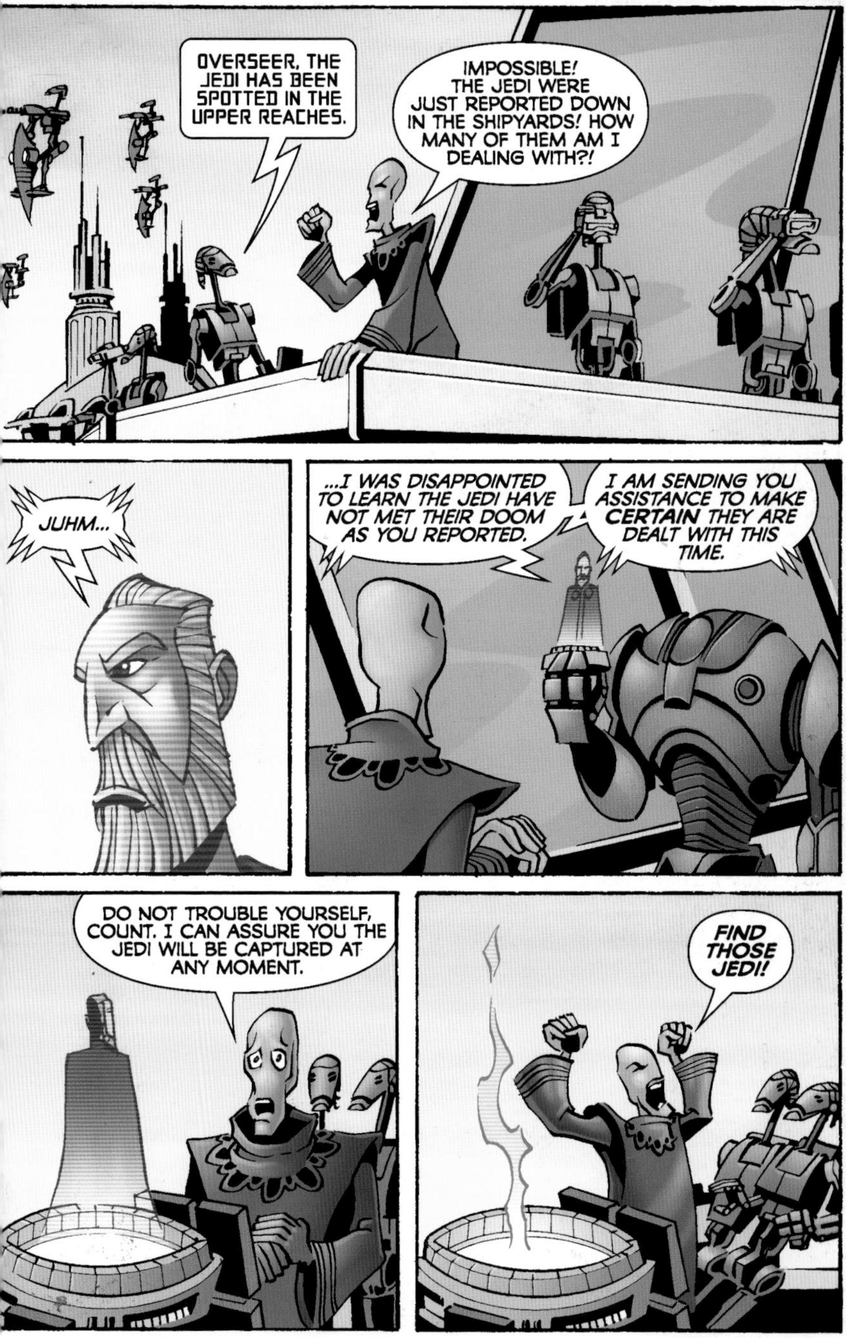
OVERSEER, THE JEDI HAS BEEN SPOTTED IN THE UPPER REACHES.
IMPOSSIBLE! THE JEDI WERE JUST REPORTED DOWN IN THE SHIPYARDS! HOW MANY OF THEM AM I DEALING WITH?!
JUHM...
...I WAS DISAPPOINTED TO LEARN THE JEDI HAVE NOT MET THEIR DOOM AS YOU REPORTED.
I AM SENDING YOU ASSISTANCE TO MAKE *CERTAIN* THEY ARE DEALT WITH THIS TIME.
DO NOT TROUBLE YOURSELF, COUNT. I CAN ASSURE YOU THE JEDI WILL BE CAPTURED AT ANY MOMENT.
FIND THOSE JEDI!

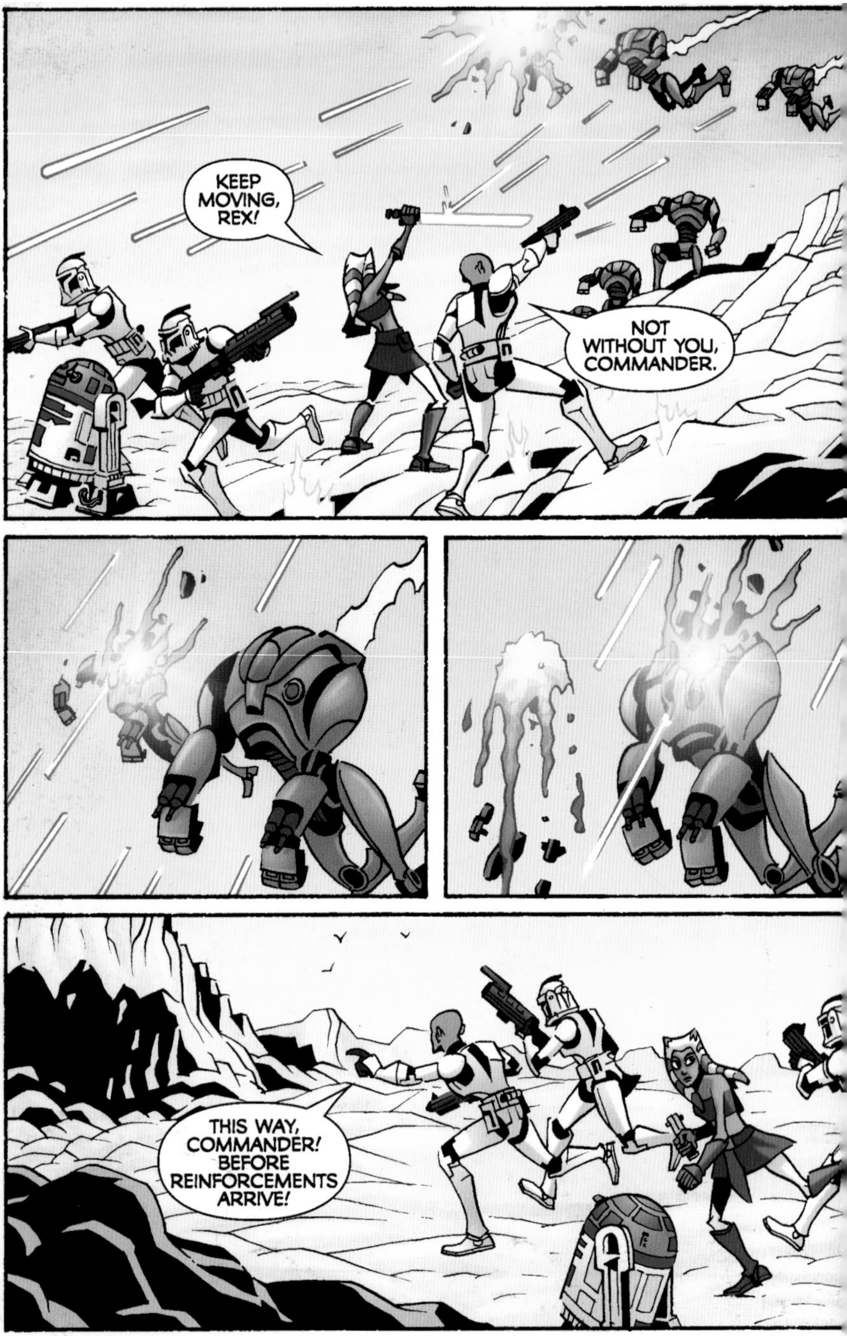
KEEP MOVING, REX!
NOT WITHOUT YOU, COMMANDER.
THIS WAY, COMMANDER! BEFORE REINFORCEMENTS ARRIVE!

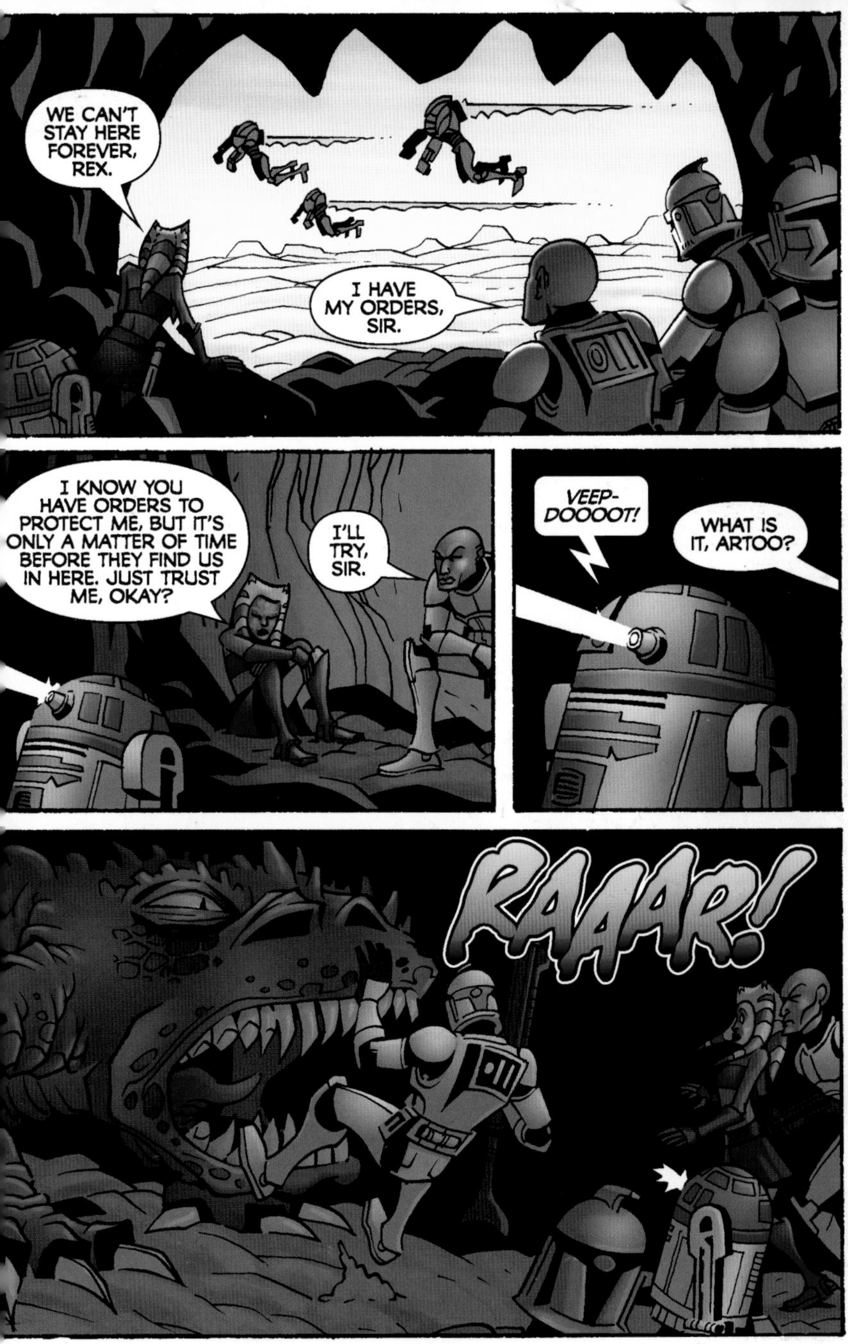
WE CAN'T STAY HERE FOREVER, REX.
I HAVE MY ORDERS, SIR.
I KNOW YOU HAVE ORDERS TO PROTECT ME, BUT IT'S ONLY A MATTER OF TIME BEFORE THEY FIND US IN HERE. JUST TRUST ME, OKAY?
I'LL TRY, SIR.
VEEP-DOOOOT!
WHAT IS IT, ARTOO?
RAAAR!

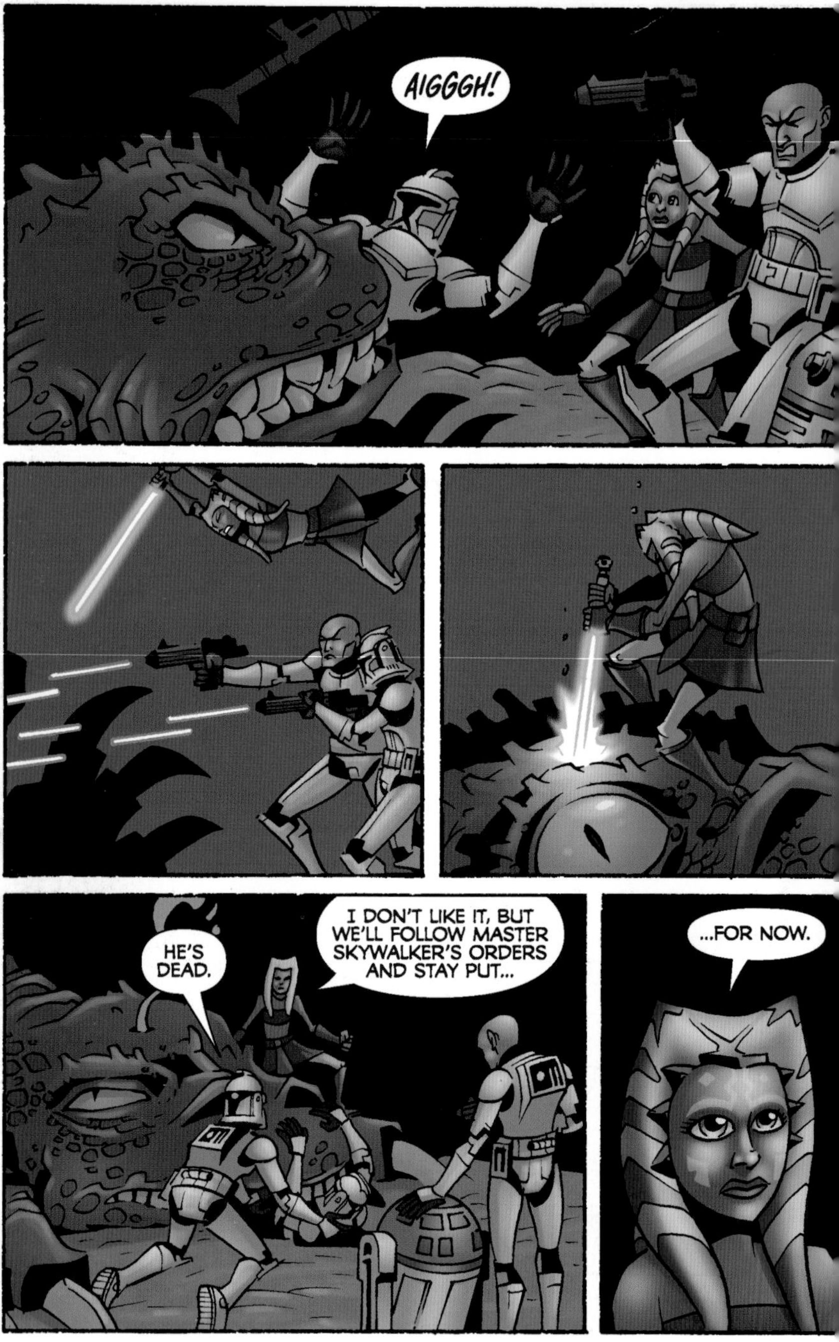
AIGGGH!
HE'S DEAD.
I DON'T LIKE IT, BUT WE'LL FOLLOW MASTER SKYWALKER'S ORDERS AND STAY PUT...
...FOR NOW.

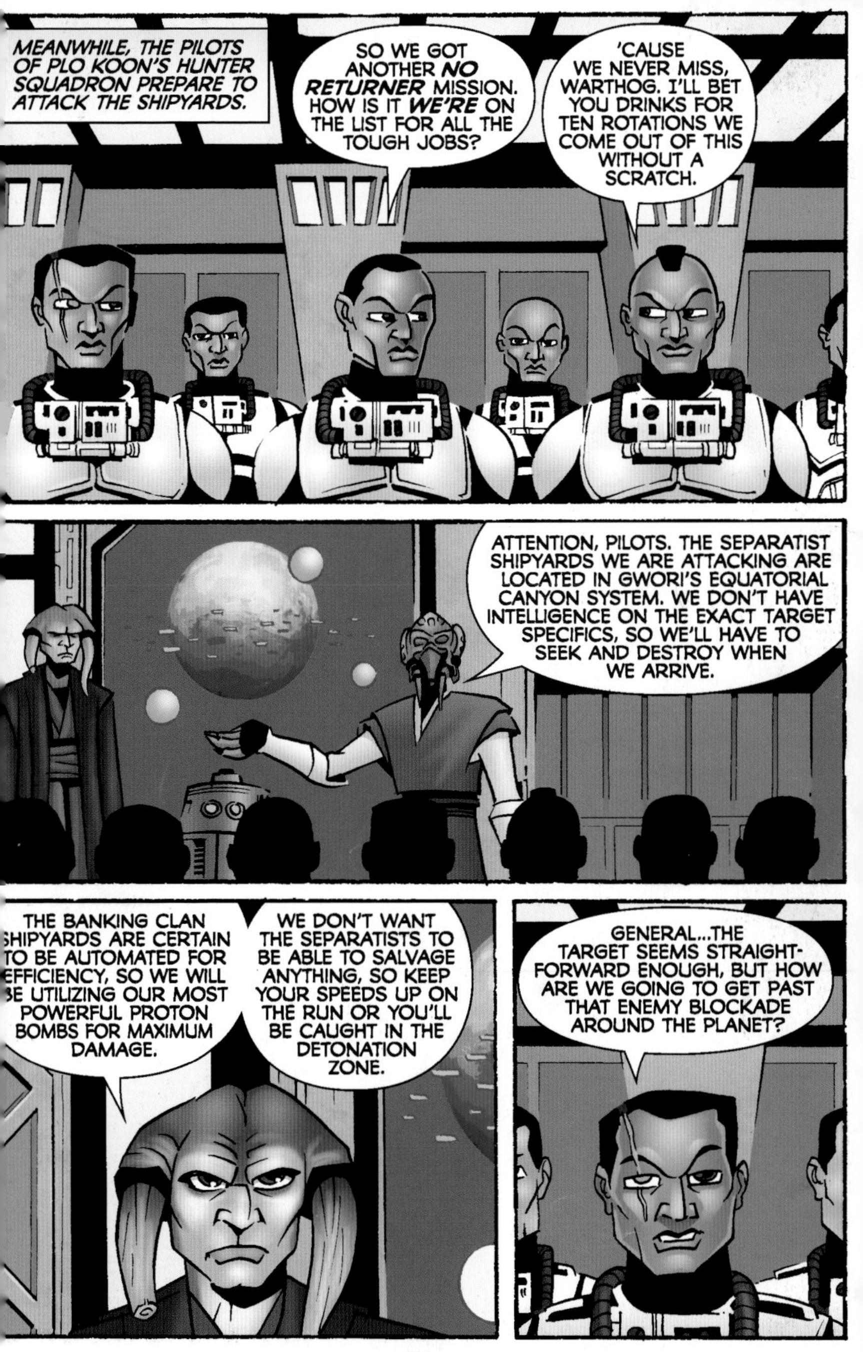
MEANWHILE, THE PILOTS OF PLO KOON'S HUNTER SQUADRON PREPARE TO ATTACK THE SHIPYARDS.
SO WE GOT ANOTHER NO RETURNER MISSION. HOW IS IT WE'RE ON THE LIST FOR ALL THE TOUGH JOBS?
'CAUSE WE NEVER MISS, WARTHOG. I'LL BET YOU DRINKS FOR TEN ROTATIONS WE COME OUT OF THIS WITHOUT A SCRATCH.
ATTENTION, PILOTS. THE SEPARATIST SHIPYARDS WE ARE ATTACKING ARE LOCATED IN GWORI'S EQUATORIAL CANYON SYSTEM. WE DON'T HAVE INTELLIGENCE ON THE EXACT TARGET SPECIFICS, SO WE'LL HAVE TO SEEK AND DESTROY WHEN WE ARRIVE.
THE BANKING CLAN SHIPYARDS ARE CERTAIN TO BE AUTOMATED FOR EFFICIENCY, SO WE WILL BE UTILIZING OUR MOST POWERFUL PROTON BOMBS FOR MAXIMUM DAMAGE.
WE DON'T WANT THE SEPARATISTS TO BE ABLE TO SALVAGE ANYTHING, SO KEEP YOUR SPEEDS UP ON THE RUN OR YOU'LL BE CAUGHT IN THE DETONATION ZONE.
GENERAL...THE TARGET SEEMS STRAIGHTFORWARD ENOUGH, BUT HOW ARE WE GOING TO GET PAST THAT ENEMY BLOCKADE AROUND THE PLANET?

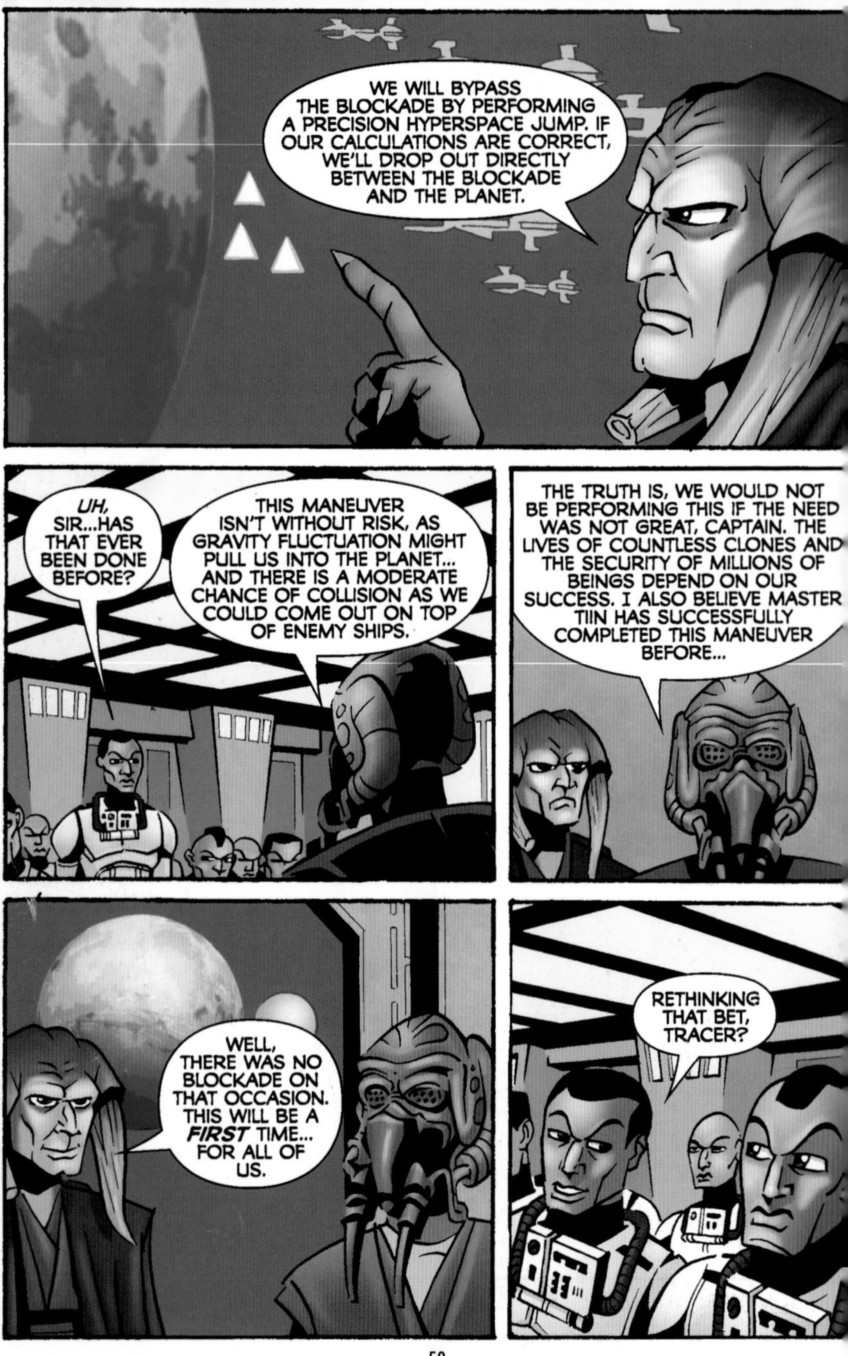
WE WILL BYPASS THE BLOCKADE BY PERFORMING A PRECISION HYPERSPACE JUMP. IF OUR CALCULATIONS ARE CORRECT, WE'LL DROP OUT DIRECTLY BETWEEN THE BLOCKADE AND THE PLANET.
UH, SIR...HAS THAT EVER BEEN DONE BEFORE?
THIS MANEUVER ISN'T WITHOUT RISK, AS GRAVITY FLUCTUATION MIGHT PULL US INTO THE PLANET... AND THERE IS A MODERATE CHANCE OF COLLISION AS WE COULD COME OUT ON TOP OF ENEMY SHIPS.
THE TRUTH IS, WE WOULD NOT BE PERFORMING THIS IF THE NEED WAS NOT GREAT, CAPTAIN. THE LIVES OF COUNTLESS CLONES AND THE SECURITY OF MILLIONS OF BEINGS DEPEND ON OUR SUCCESS. I ALSO BELIEVE MASTER TIIN HAS SUCCESSFULLY COMPLETED THIS MANEUVER BEFORE...
WELL, THERE WAS NO BLOCKADE ON THAT OCCASION. THIS WILL BE A ***FIRST*** TIME... FOR ALL OF US.
RETHINKING THAT BET, TRACER?

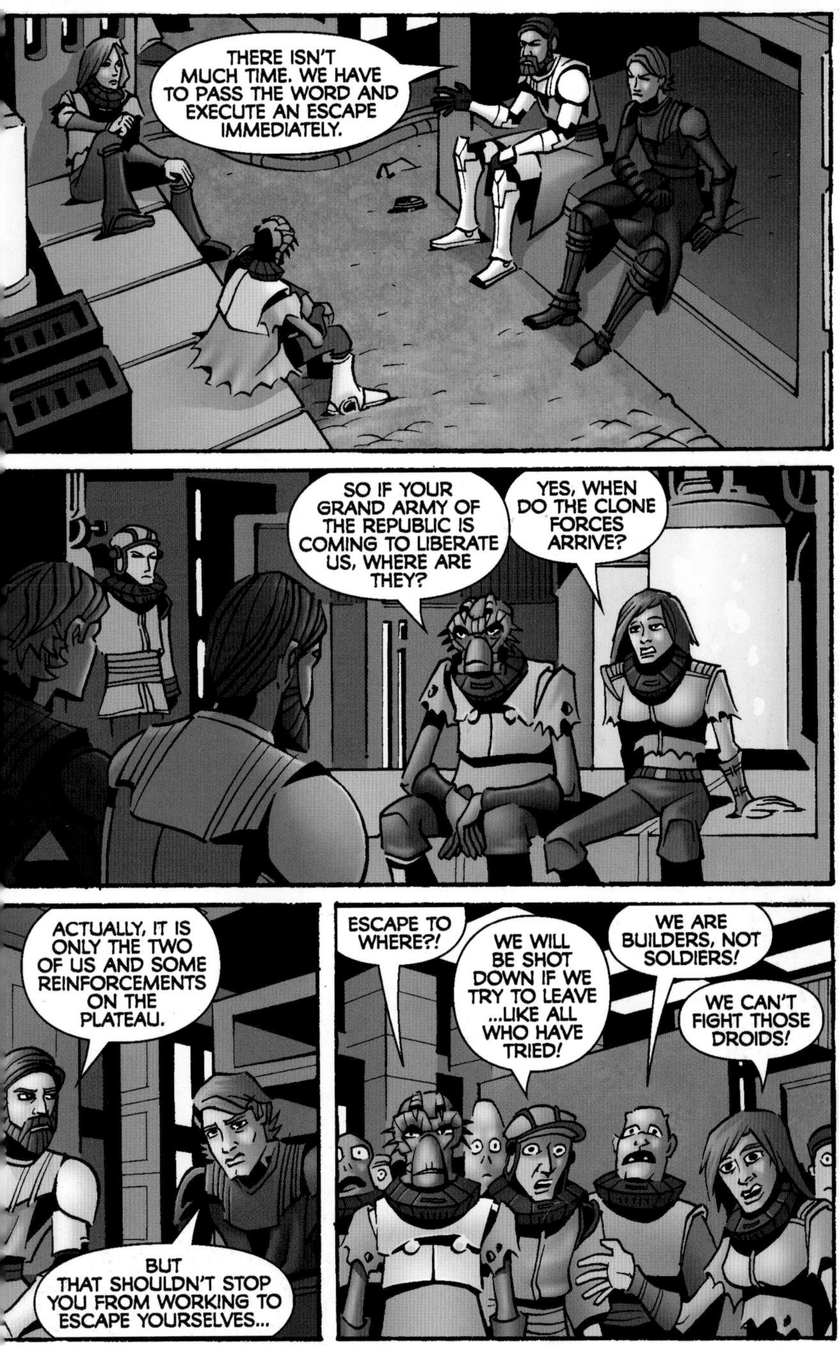
THERE ISN'T MUCH TIME. WE HAVE TO PASS THE WORD AND EXECUTE AN ESCAPE IMMEDIATELY.
SO IF YOUR GRAND ARMY OF THE REPUBLIC IS COMING TO LIBERATE US, WHERE ARE THEY?
YES, WHEN DO THE CLONE FORCES ARRIVE?
ACTUALLY, IT IS ONLY THE TWO OF US AND SOME REINFORCEMENTS ON THE PLATEAU.
BUT THAT SHOULDN'T STOP YOU FROM WORKING TO ESCAPE YOURSELVES...
ESCAPE TO WHERE?!
WE WILL BE SHOT DOWN IF WE TRY TO LEAVE ...LIKE ALL WHO HAVE TRIED!
WE ARE BUILDERS, NOT SOLDIERS!
WE CAN'T FIGHT THOSE DROIDS!

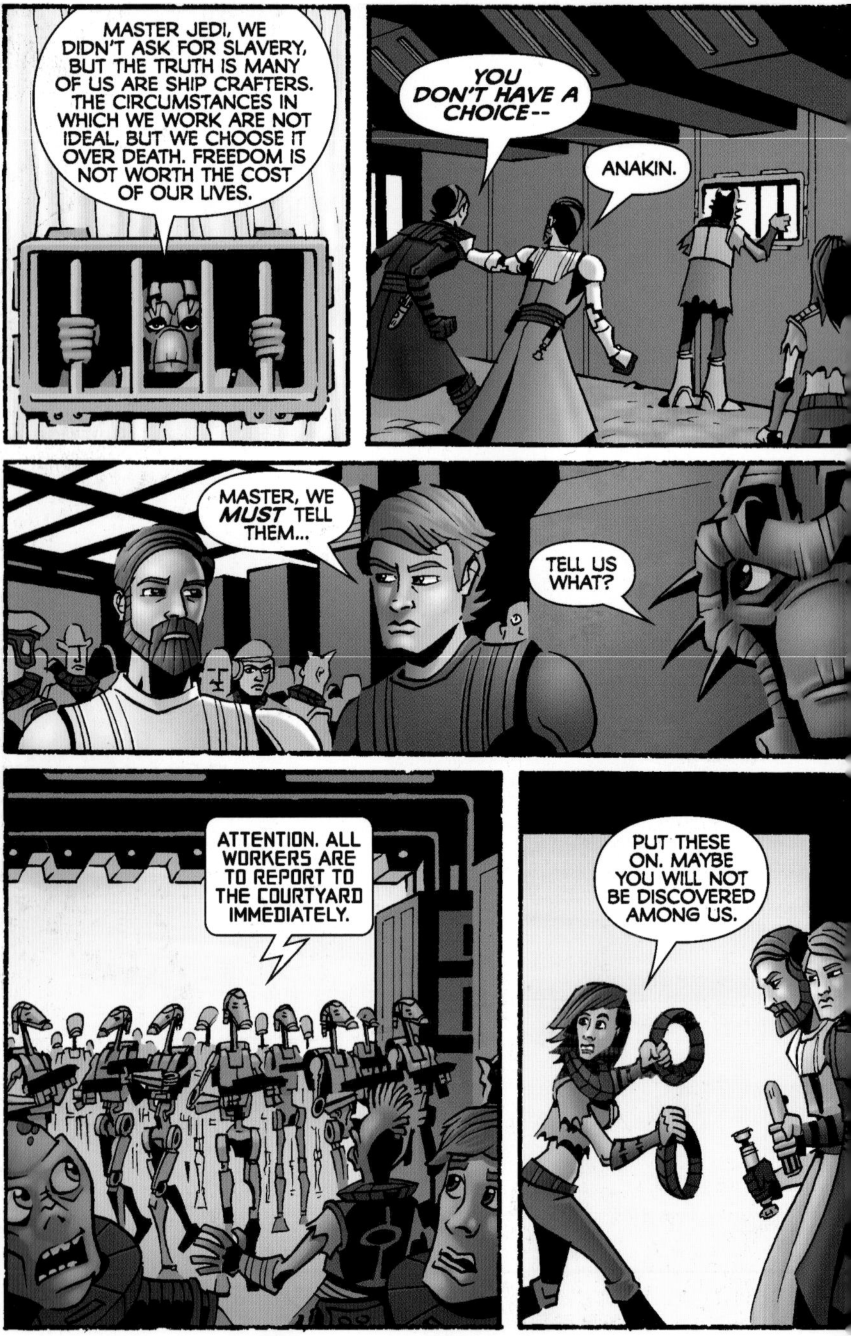

MASTER JEDI, WE DIDN'T ASK FOR SLAVERY, BUT THE TRUTH IS MANY OF US ARE SHIP CRAFTERS. THE CIRCUMSTANCES IN WHICH WE WORK ARE NOT IDEAL, BUT WE CHOOSE IT OVER DEATH. FREEDOM IS NOT WORTH THE COST OF OUR LIVES.
YOU DON'T HAVE A CHOICE--
ANAKIN.
MASTER, WE MUST TELL THEM...
TELL US WHAT?
ATTENTION. ALL WORKERS ARE TO REPORT TO THE COURTYARD IMMEDIATELY.
PUT THESE ON. MAYBE YOU WILL NOT BE DISCOVERED AMONG US.

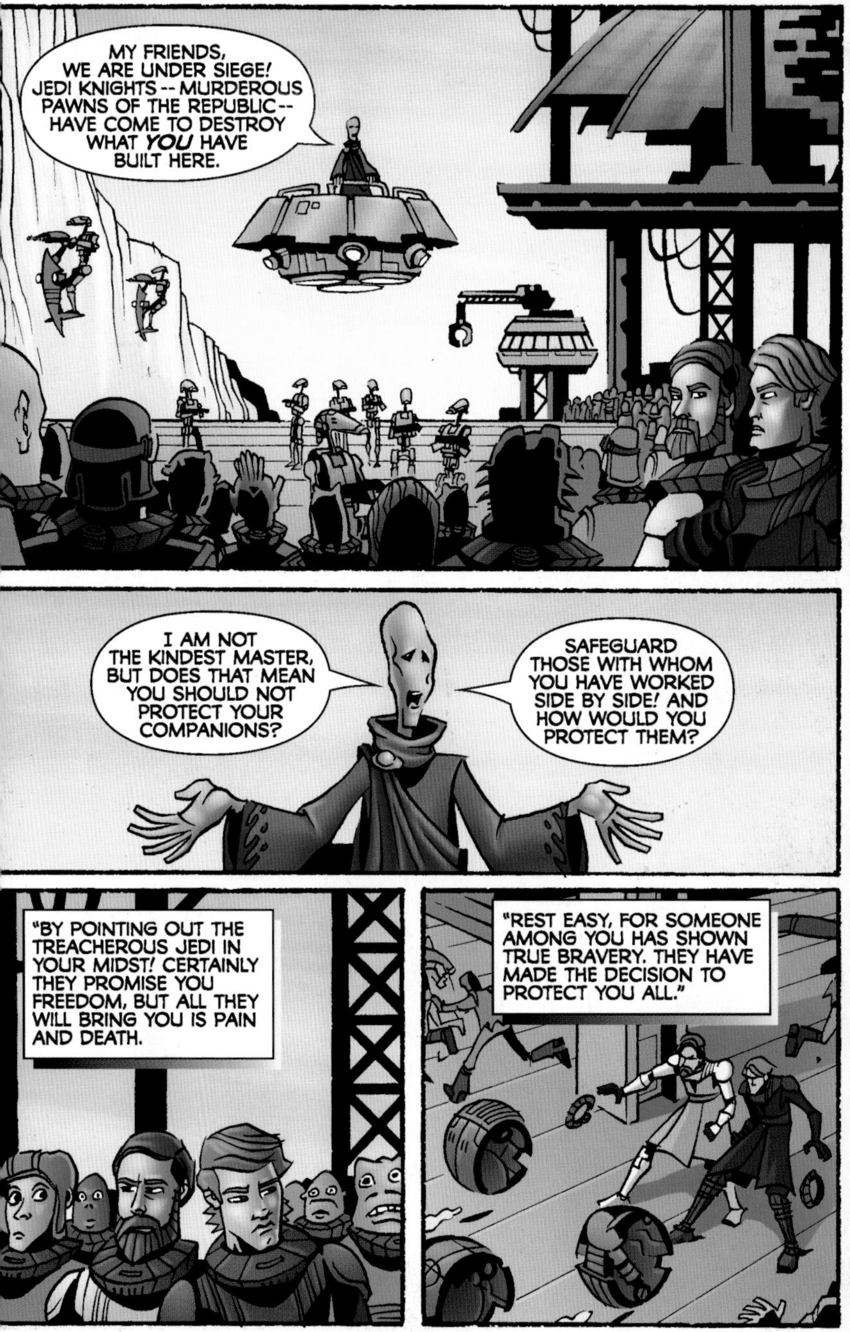
MY FRIENDS, WE ARE UNDER SIEGE! JEDI KNIGHTS -- MURDEROUS PAWNS OF THE REPUBLIC -- HAVE COME TO DESTROY WHAT *YOU* HAVE BUILT HERE.
I AM NOT THE KINDEST MASTER, BUT DOES THAT MEAN YOU SHOULD NOT PROTECT YOUR COMPANIONS?
SAFEGUARD THOSE WITH WHOM YOU HAVE WORKED SIDE BY SIDE! AND HOW WOULD YOU PROTECT THEM?
"BY POINTING OUT THE TREACHEROUS JEDI IN YOUR MIDST! CERTAINLY THEY PROMISE YOU FREEDOM, BUT ALL THEY WILL BRING YOU IS PAIN AND DEATH.
"REST EASY, FOR SOMEONE AMONG YOU HAS SHOWN TRUE BRAVERY. THEY HAVE MADE THE DECISION TO PROTECT YOU ALL."

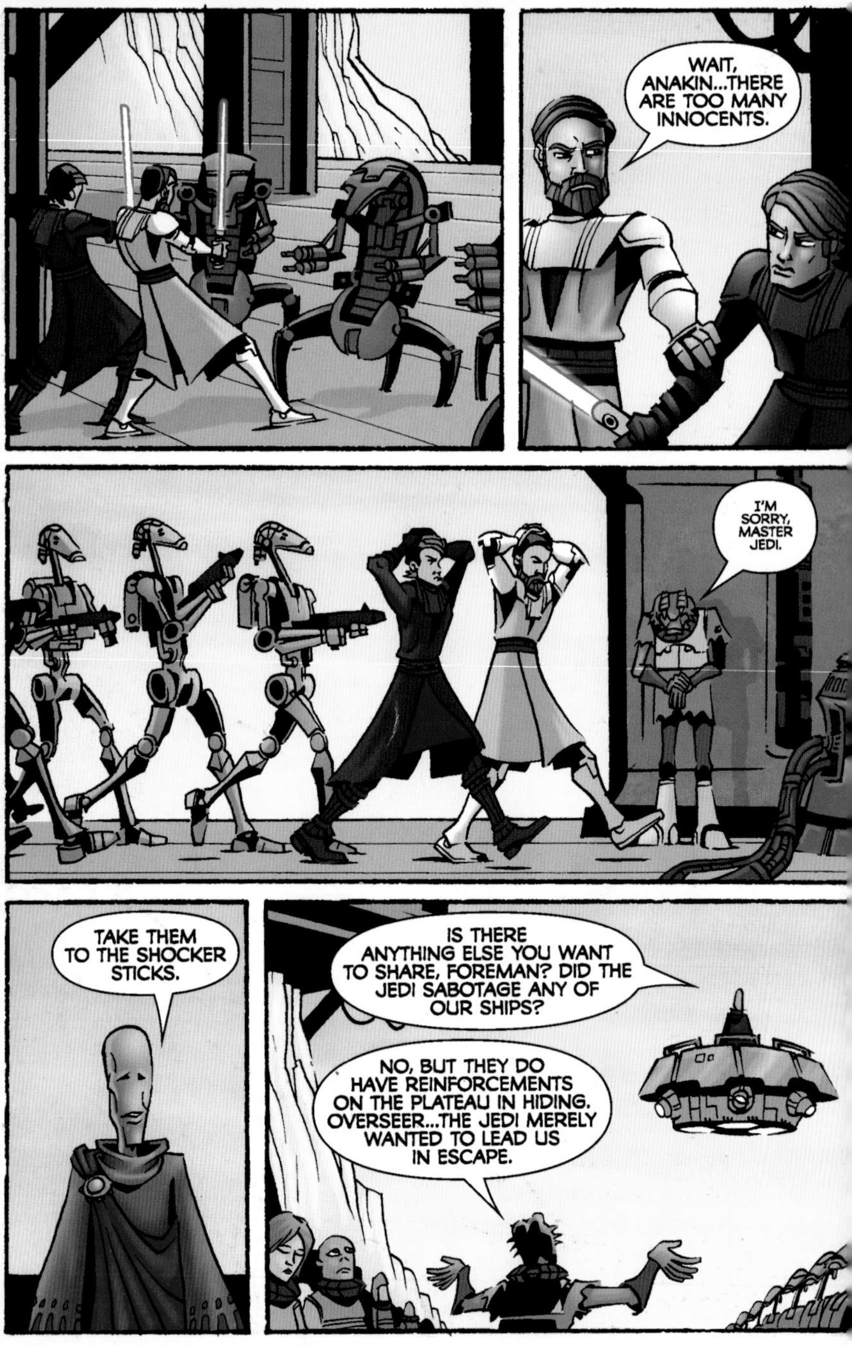
WAIT, ANAKIN...THERE ARE TOO MANY INNOCENTS.
I'M SORRY, MASTER JEDI.
TAKE THEM TO THE SHOCKER STICKS.
IS THERE ANYTHING ELSE YOU WANT TO SHARE, FOREMAN? DID THE JEDI SABOTAGE ANY OF OUR SHIPS?
NO, BUT THEY DO HAVE REINFORCEMENTS ON THE PLATEAU IN HIDING. OVERSEER...THE JEDI MERELY WANTED TO LEAD US IN ESCAPE.

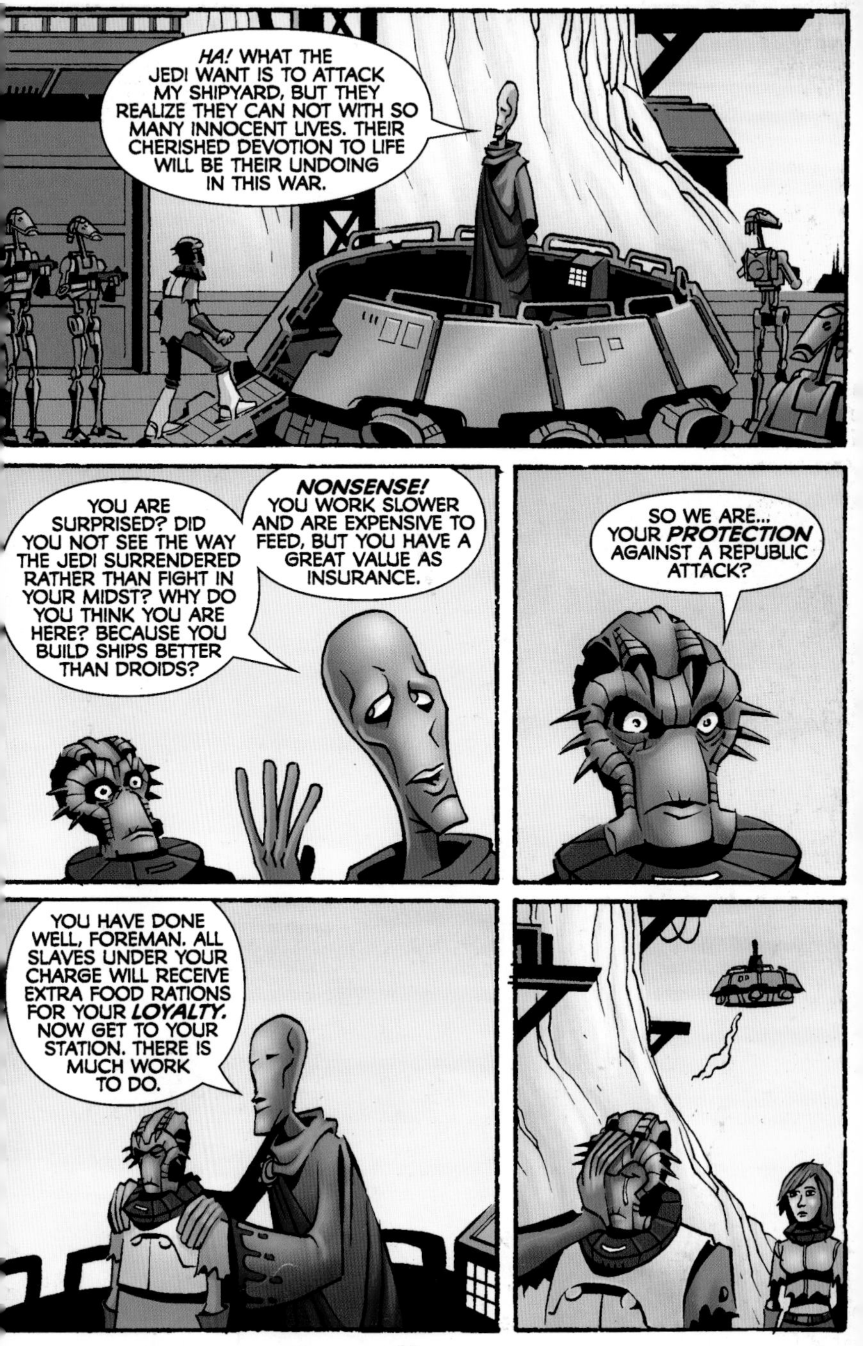
HA! WHAT THE JEDI WANT IS TO ATTACK MY SHIPYARD, BUT THEY REALIZE THEY CAN NOT WITH SO MANY INNOCENT LIVES. THEIR CHERISHED DEVOTION TO LIFE WILL BE THEIR UNDOING IN THIS WAR.
YOU ARE SURPRISED? DID YOU NOT SEE THE WAY THE JEDI SURRENDERED RATHER THAN FIGHT IN YOUR MIDST? WHY DO YOU THINK YOU ARE HERE? BECAUSE YOU BUILD SHIPS BETTER THAN DROIDS?
NONSENSE! YOU WORK SLOWER AND ARE EXPENSIVE TO FEED, BUT YOU HAVE A GREAT VALUE AS INSURANCE.
SO WE ARE... YOUR PROTECTION AGAINST A REPUBLIC ATTACK?
YOU HAVE DONE WELL, FOREMAN. ALL SLAVES UNDER YOUR CHARGE WILL RECEIVE EXTRA FOOD RATIONS FOR YOUR LOYALTY. NOW GET TO YOUR STATION. THERE IS MUCH WORK TO DO.

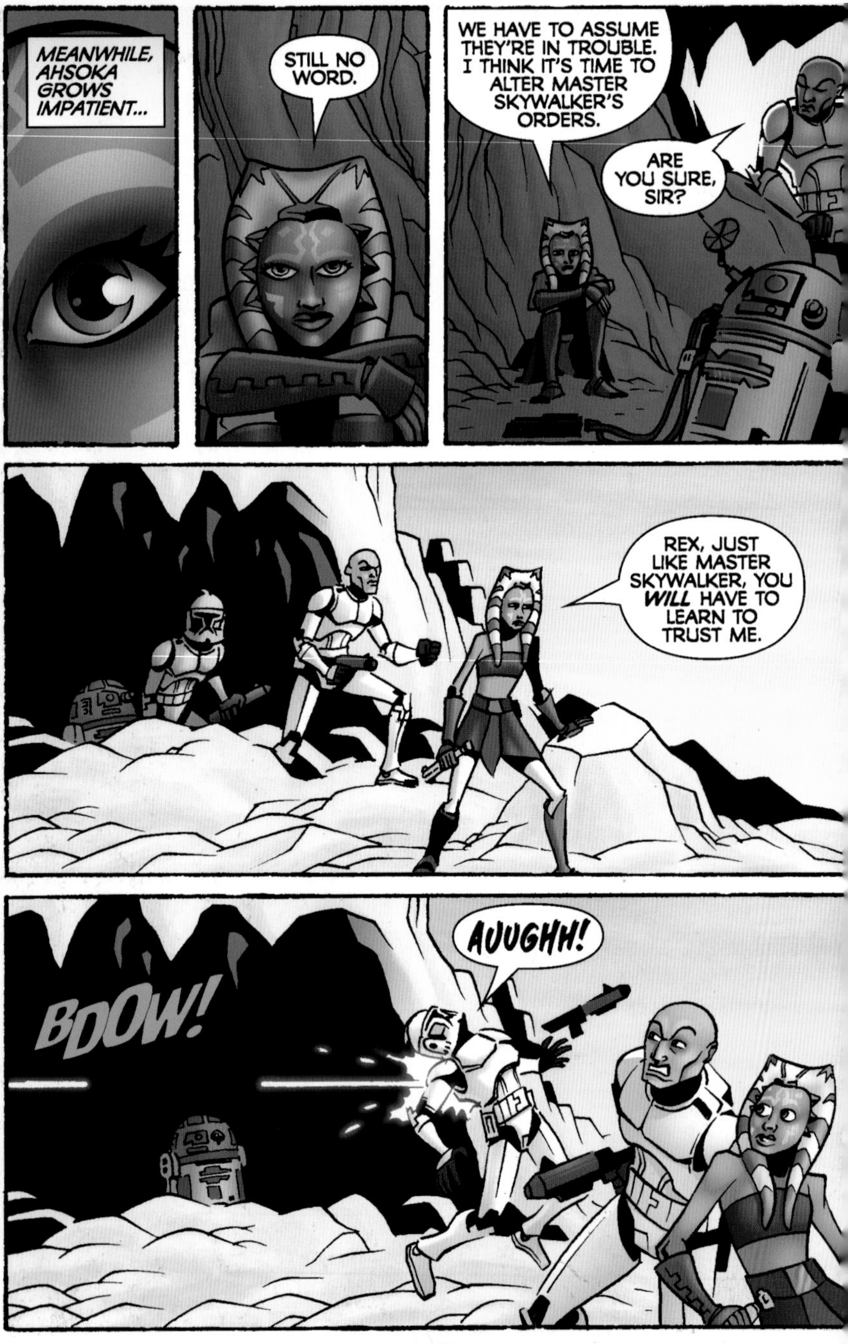
MEANWHILE, AHSOKA GROWS IMPATIENT...
STILL NO WORD.
WE HAVE TO ASSUME THEY'RE IN TROUBLE. I THINK IT'S TIME TO ALTER MASTER SKYWALKER'S ORDERS.
ARE YOU SURE, SIR?
REX, JUST LIKE MASTER SKYWALKER, YOU *WILL* HAVE TO LEARN TO TRUST ME.
AUUGHH!
BDOW!

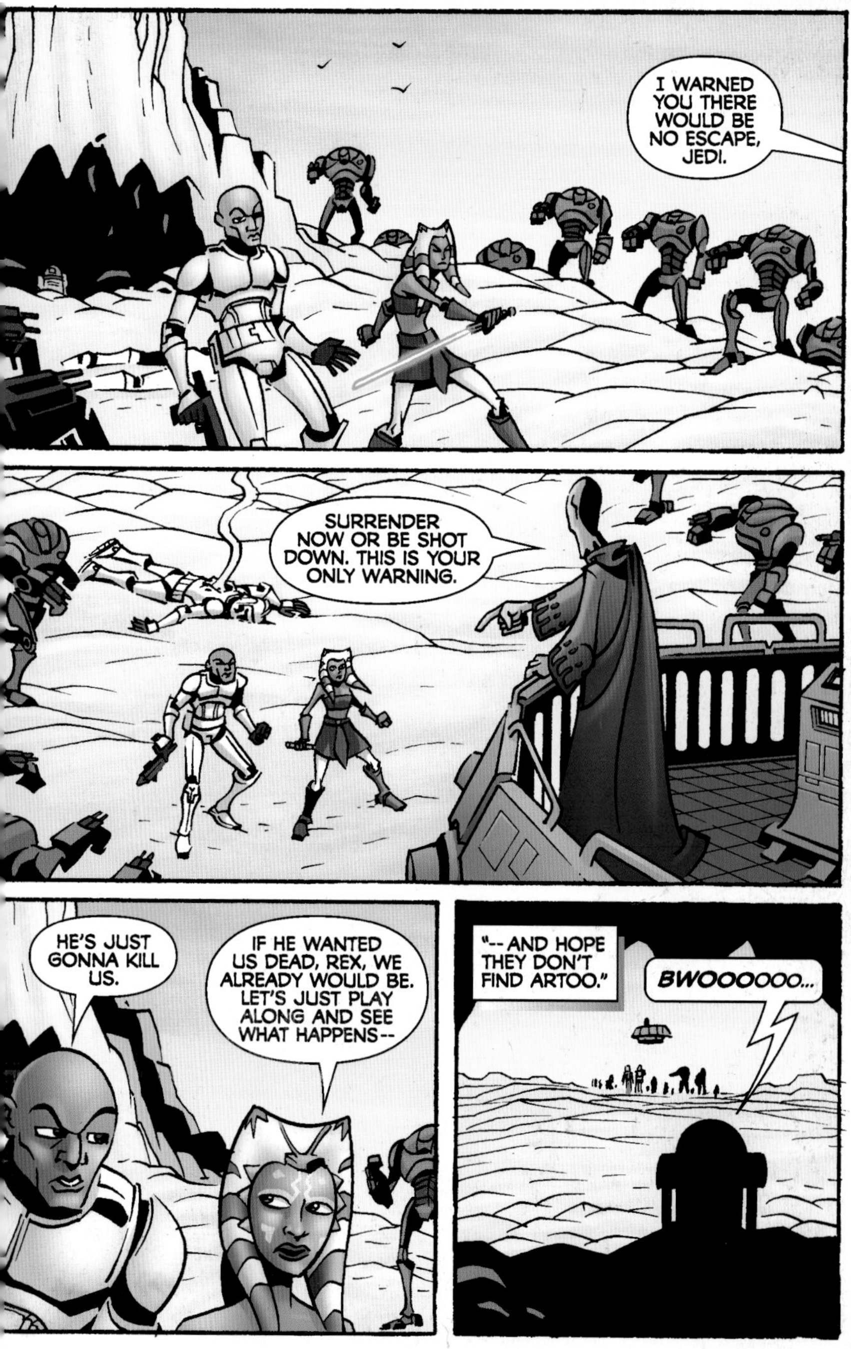
I WARNED YOU THERE WOULD BE NO ESCAPE, JEDI.
SURRENDER NOW OR BE SHOT DOWN. THIS IS YOUR ONLY WARNING.
HE'S JUST GONNA KILL US.
IF HE WANTED US DEAD, REX, WE ALREADY WOULD BE. LET'S JUST PLAY ALONG AND SEE WHAT HAPPENS--
"--AND HOPE THEY DON'T FIND ARTOO."
BWOOOOOO...

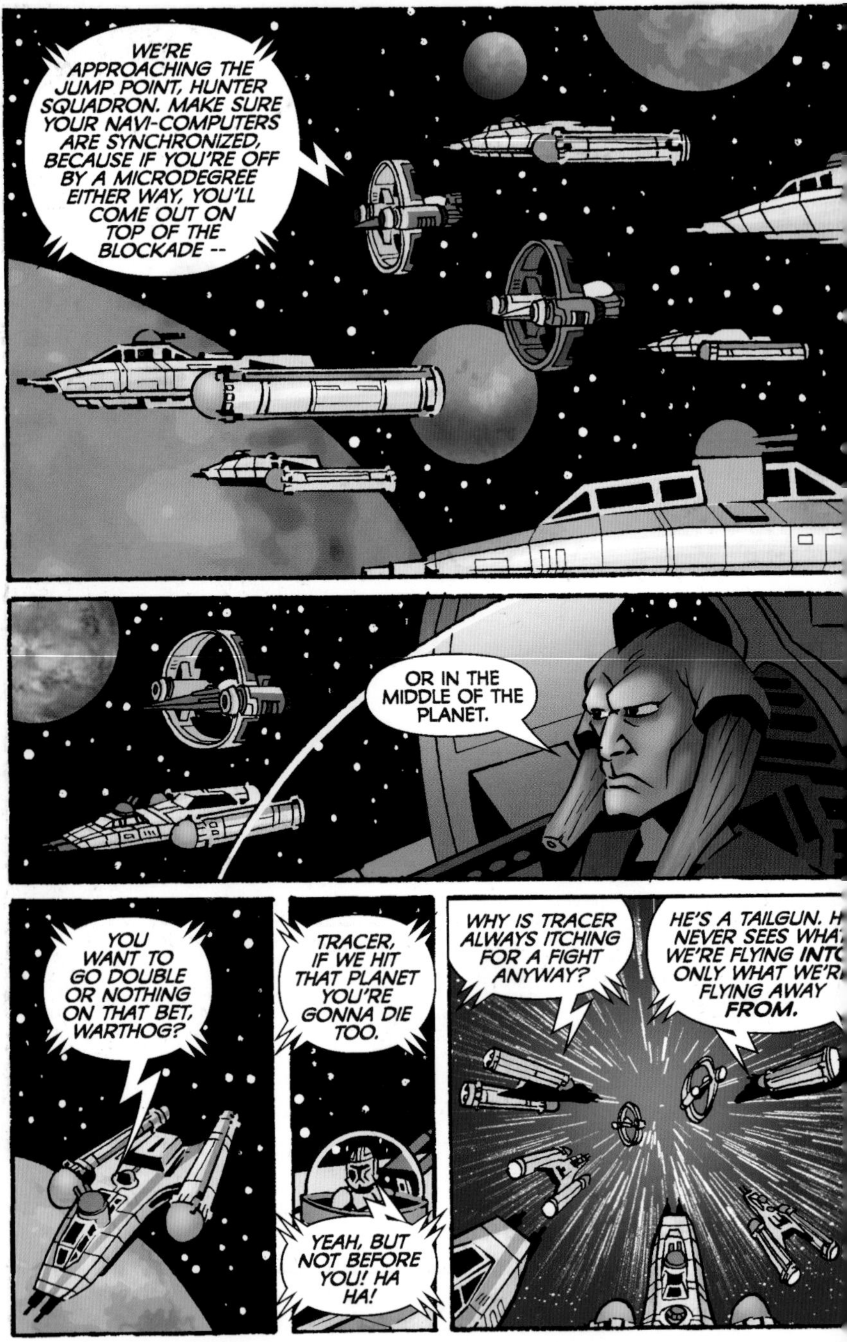

WE'RE APPROACHING THE JUMP POINT, HUNTER SQUADRON. MAKE SURE YOUR NAVI-COMPUTERS ARE SYNCHRONIZED, BECAUSE IF YOU'RE OFF BY A MICRODEGREE EITHER WAY, YOU'LL COME OUT ON TOP OF THE BLOCKADE --
OR IN THE MIDDLE OF THE PLANET.
YOU WANT TO GO DOUBLE OR NOTHING ON THAT BET, WARTHOG?
TRACER, IF WE HIT THAT PLANET YOU'RE GONNA DIE TOO.
YEAH, BUT NOT BEFORE YOU! HA HA!
WHY IS TRACER ALWAYS ITCHING FOR A FIGHT ANYWAY?

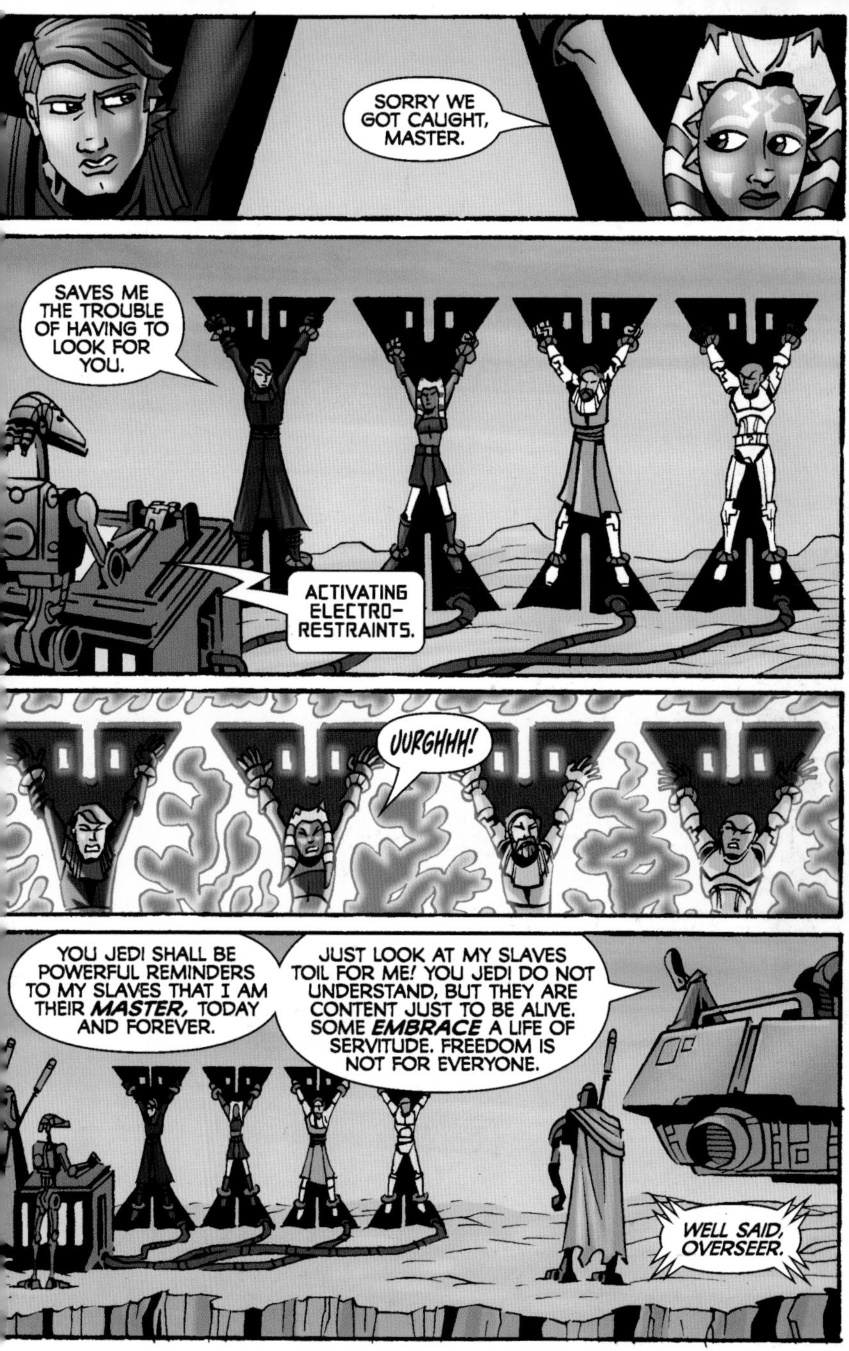
SORRY WE GOT CAUGHT, MASTER.
SAVES ME THE TROUBLE OF HAVING TO LOOK FOR YOU.
ACTIVATING ELECTRO-RESTRAINTS.
UURGHHH!
YOU JEDI SHALL BE POWERFUL REMINDERS TO MY SLAVES THAT I AM THEIR *MASTER,* TODAY AND FOREVER.
JUST LOOK AT MY SLAVES TOIL FOR ME! YOU JEDI DO NOT UNDERSTAND, BUT THEY ARE CONTENT JUST TO BE ALIVE. SOME *EMBRACE* A LIFE OF SERVITUDE. FREEDOM IS NOT FOR EVERYONE.
WELL SAID, OVERSEER.

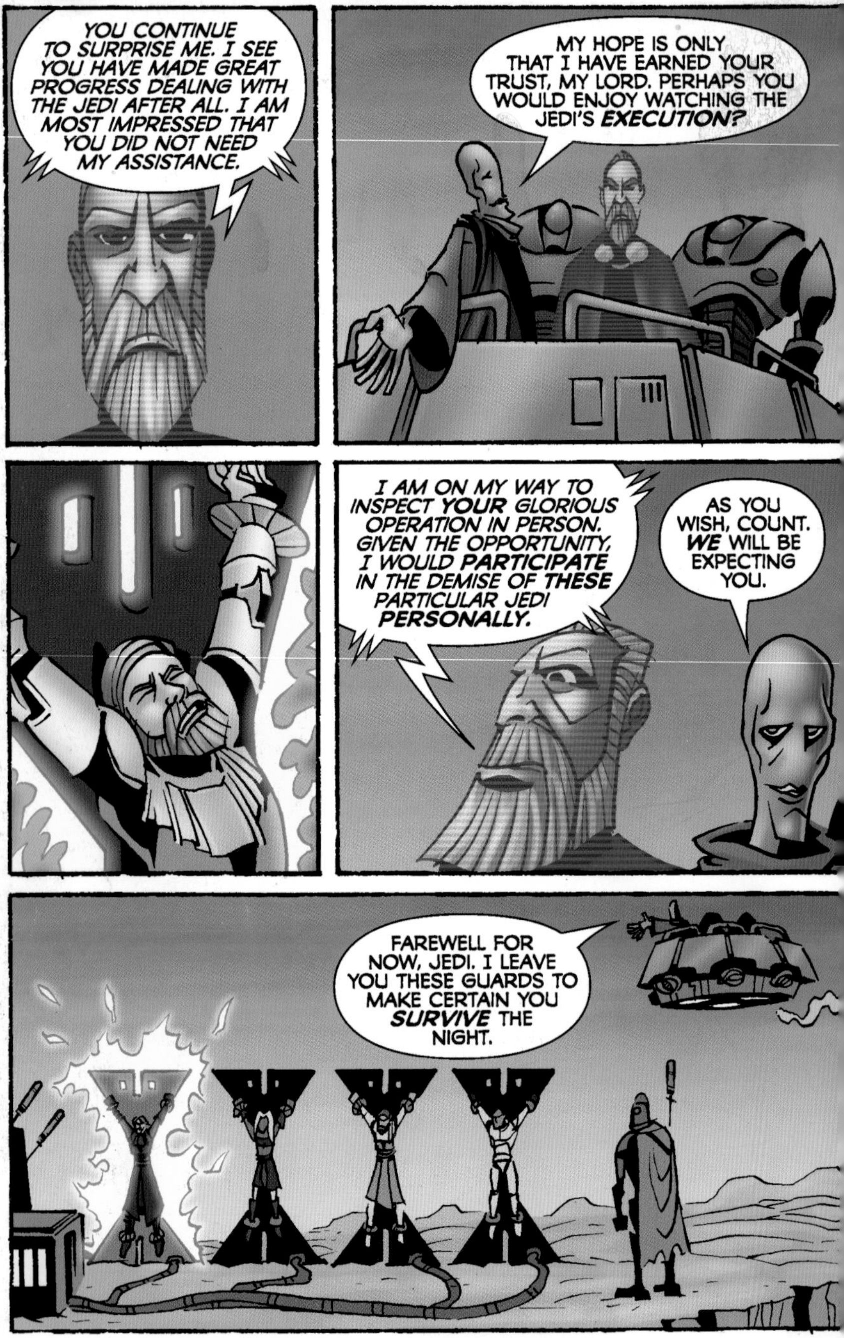
YOU CONTINUE TO SURPRISE ME. I SEE YOU HAVE MADE GREAT PROGRESS DEALING WITH THE JEDI AFTER ALL. I AM MOST IMPRESSED THAT YOU DID NOT NEED MY ASSISTANCE.
MY HOPE IS ONLY THAT I HAVE EARNED YOUR TRUST, MY LORD. PERHAPS YOU WOULD ENJOY WATCHING THE JEDI'S ***EXECUTION?***
I AM ON MY WAY TO INSPECT **YOUR** GLORIOUS OPERATION IN PERSON. GIVEN THE OPPORTUNITY, I WOULD **PARTICIPATE** IN THE DEMISE OF **THESE** PARTICULAR JEDI **PERSONALLY.**
AS YOU WISH, COUNT. ***WE*** WILL BE EXPECTING YOU.
FAREWELL FOR NOW, JEDI. I LEAVE YOU THESE GUARDS TO MAKE CERTAIN YOU ***SURVIVE*** THE NIGHT.

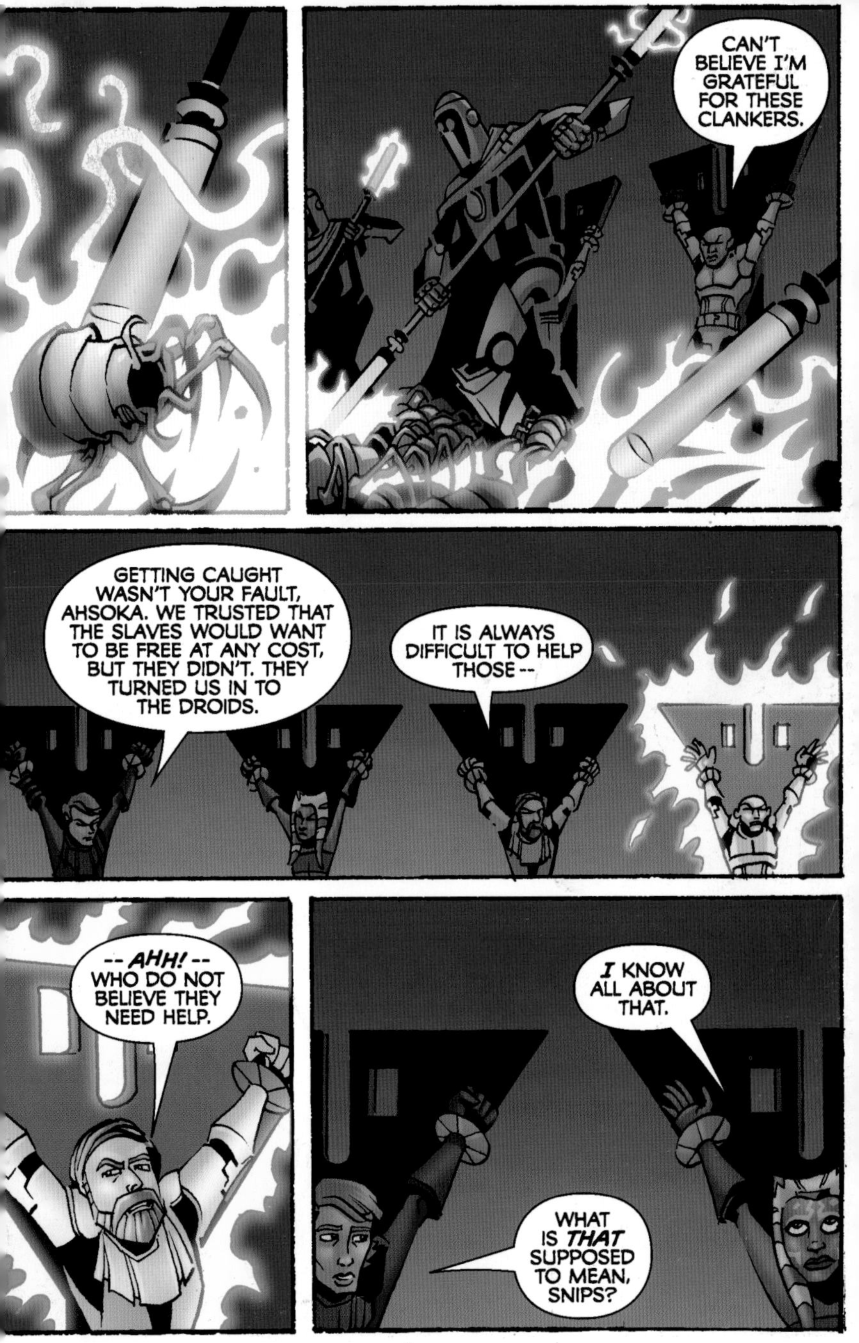
CAN'T BELIEVE I'M GRATEFUL FOR THESE CLANKERS.
GETTING CAUGHT WASN'T YOUR FAULT, AHSOKA. WE TRUSTED THAT THE SLAVES WOULD WANT TO BE FREE AT ANY COST, BUT THEY DIDN'T. THEY TURNED US IN TO THE DROIDS.
IT IS ALWAYS DIFFICULT TO HELP THOSE --
-- *AHH!* -- WHO DO NOT BELIEVE THEY NEED HELP.
I KNOW ALL ABOUT THAT.
WHAT IS *THAT* SUPPOSED TO MEAN, SNIPS?

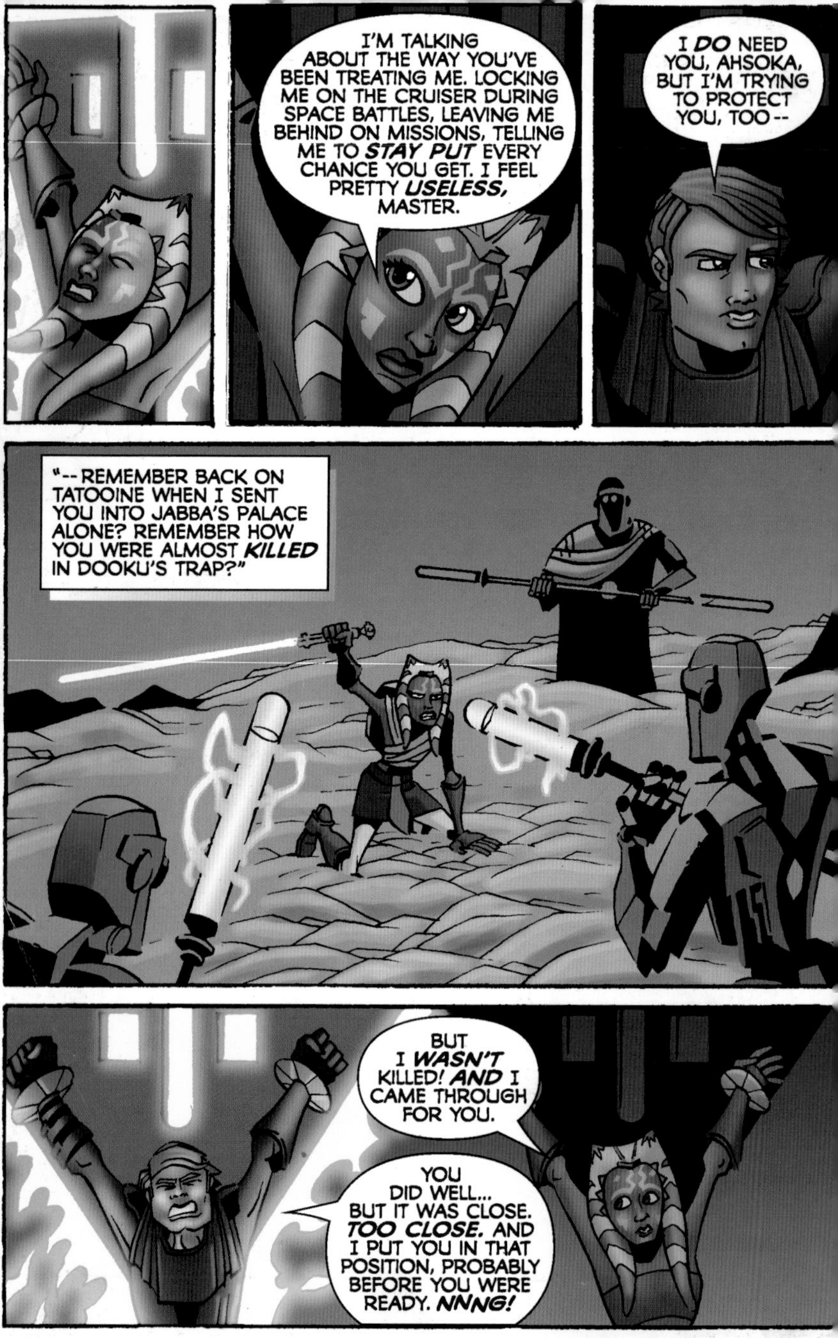
I'M TALKING ABOUT THE WAY YOU'VE BEEN TREATING ME. LOCKING ME ON THE CRUISER DURING SPACE BATTLES, LEAVING ME BEHIND ON MISSIONS, TELLING ME TO STAY PUT EVERY CHANCE YOU GET. I FEEL PRETTY USELESS, MASTER.
I DO NEED YOU, AHSOKA, BUT I'M TRYING TO PROTECT YOU, TOO --
"-- REMEMBER BACK ON TATOOINE WHEN I SENT YOU INTO JABBA'S PALACE ALONE? REMEMBER HOW YOU WERE ALMOST KILLED IN DOOKU'S TRAP?"
BUT I WASN'T KILLED! AND I CAME THROUGH FOR YOU.
YOU DID WELL... BUT IT WAS CLOSE. TOO CLOSE. AND I PUT YOU IN THAT POSITION, PROBABLY BEFORE YOU WERE READY. NNNG!

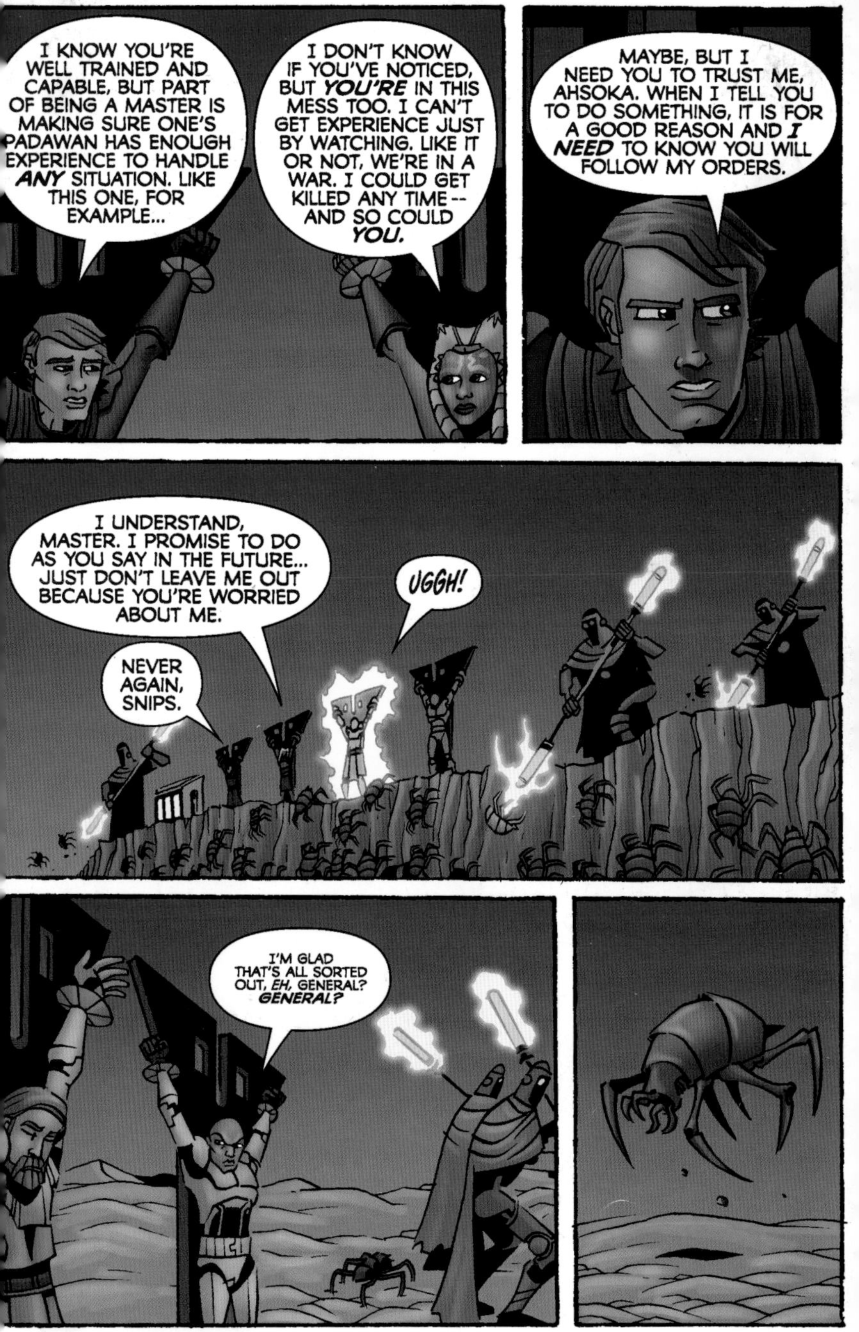
I KNOW YOU'RE WELL TRAINED AND CAPABLE, BUT PART OF BEING A MASTER IS MAKING SURE ONE'S PADAWAN HAS ENOUGH EXPERIENCE TO HANDLE ANY SITUATION. LIKE THIS ONE, FOR EXAMPLE...
I DON'T KNOW IF YOU'VE NOTICED, BUT YOU'RE IN THIS MESS TOO. I CAN'T GET EXPERIENCE JUST BY WATCHING. LIKE IT OR NOT, WE'RE IN A WAR. I COULD GET KILLED ANY TIME -- AND SO COULD YOU.
MAYBE, BUT I NEED YOU TO TRUST ME, AHSOKA. WHEN I TELL YOU TO DO SOMETHING, IT IS FOR A GOOD REASON AND I NEED TO KNOW YOU WILL FOLLOW MY ORDERS.
I UNDERSTAND, MASTER. I PROMISE TO DO AS YOU SAY IN THE FUTURE... JUST DON'T LEAVE ME OUT BECAUSE YOU'RE WORRIED ABOUT ME.
NEVER AGAIN, SNIPS.
UGGH!
I'M GLAD THAT'S ALL SORTED OUT, EH, GENERAL? GENERAL?

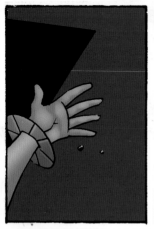

GREAT IDEA, MASTER, I KNEW I BROUGHT YOU ALONG FOR A GOOD REASON!

KRSSH!

AHSOKA, SEE THAT CREATURE CLOSEST TO US?

ALREADY ON IT!

"TOGETHER NOW..."

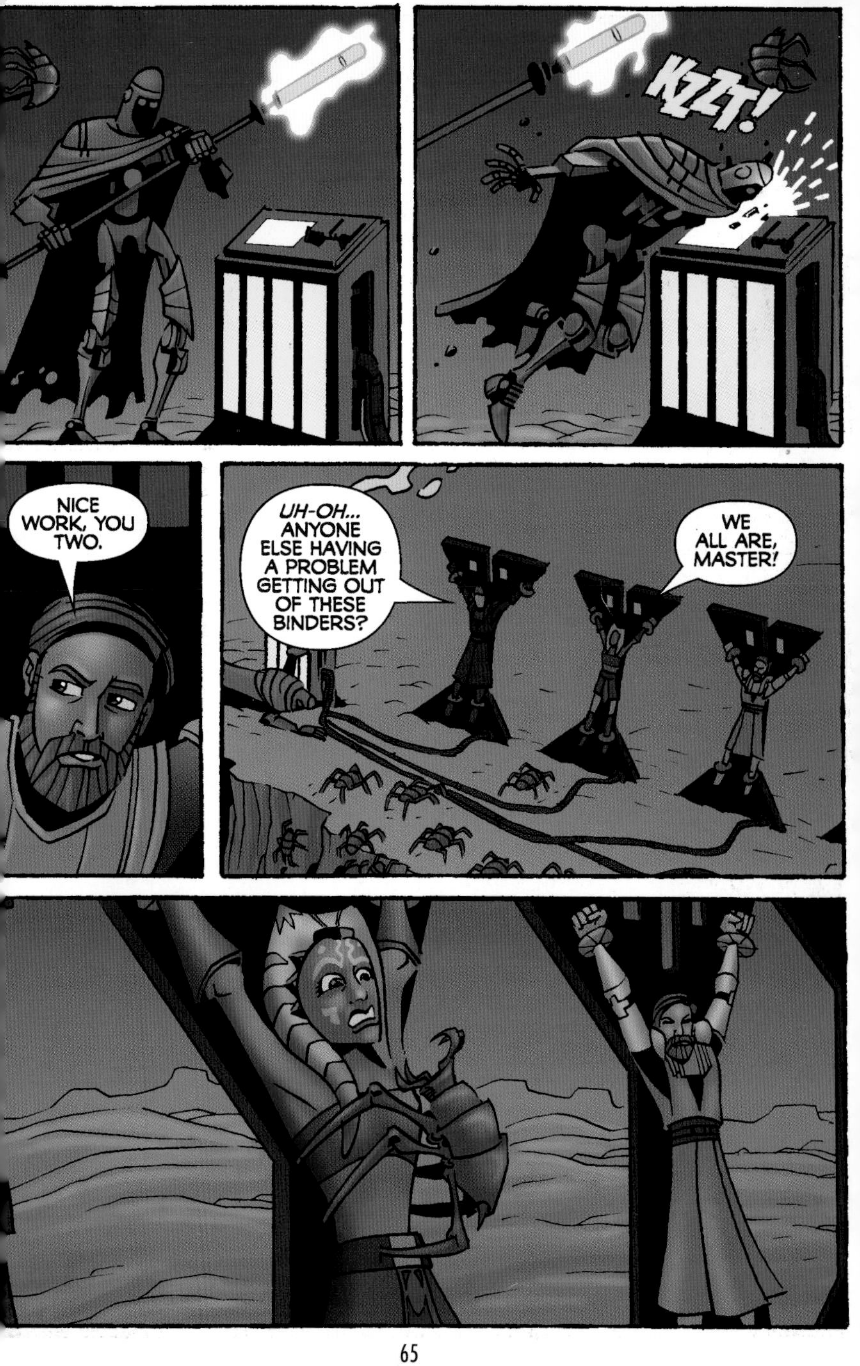
KZZT!
NICE WORK, YOU TWO.
UH-OH... ANYONE ELSE HAVING A PROBLEM GETTING OUT OF THESE BINDERS?
WE ALL ARE, MASTER!

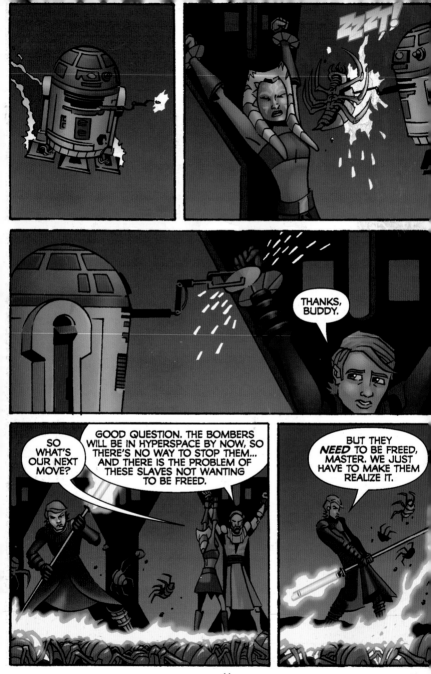

ZZT!

THANKS, BUDDY.

SO WHAT'S OUR NEXT MOVE?

GOOD QUESTION. THE BOMBERS WILL BE IN HYPERSPACE BY NOW, SO THERE'S NO WAY TO STOP THEM... AND THERE IS THE PROBLEM OF THESE SLAVES NOT WANTING TO BE FREED.

BUT THEY *NEED* TO BE FREED, MASTER. WE JUST HAVE TO MAKE THEM REALIZE IT.

YOU DON'T SLEEP, MIRAX. PERHAPS YOUR CONSCIENCE HAUNTS YOU FOR SENDING THOSE JEDI TO THEIR DEATHS?

WHAT WAS I TO DO? GET US ALL SHOT TRYING TO FIGHT THE DROIDS?

THERE ARE ALTERNATIVES TO FIGHTING.

THE JEDI!

YOU HAVE RETURNED!

TO OFFER YOU A SECOND CHANCE AT FREEDOM. AT THIS MOMENT, REPUBLIC BOMBERS ARE ON THEIR WAY TO DESTROY THE SHIPYARDS. THERE'S NO WAY TO STOP THEM--

EXCEPT BY WARNING OVERSEER JUHM.

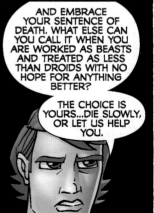

AND EMBRACE YOUR SENTENCE OF DEATH. WHAT ELSE CAN YOU CALL IT WHEN YOU ARE WORKED AS BEASTS AND TREATED AS LESS THAN DROIDS WITH NO HOPE FOR ANYTHING BETTER?

THE CHOICE IS YOURS...DIE SLOWLY, OR LET US HELP YOU.

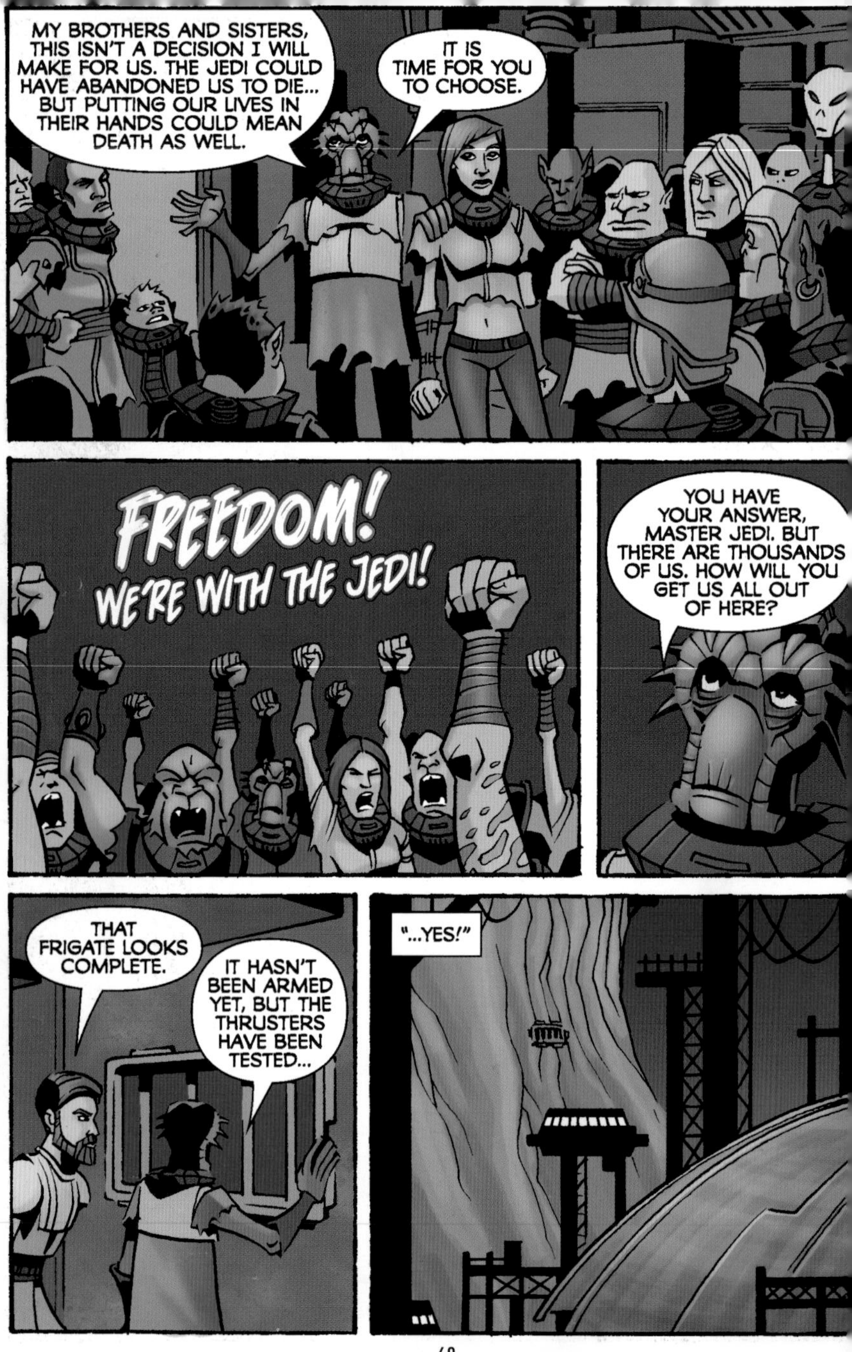
MY BROTHERS AND SISTERS, THIS ISN'T A DECISION I WILL MAKE FOR US. THE JEDI COULD HAVE ABANDONED US TO DIE... BUT PUTTING OUR LIVES IN THEIR HANDS COULD MEAN DEATH AS WELL.
IT IS TIME FOR YOU TO CHOOSE.
FREEDOM!
WE'RE WITH THE JEDI!
YOU HAVE YOUR ANSWER, MASTER JEDI. BUT THERE ARE THOUSANDS OF US. HOW WILL YOU GET US ALL OUT OF HERE?
THAT FRIGATE LOOKS COMPLETE.
IT HASN'T BEEN ARMED YET, BUT THE THRUSTERS HAVE BEEN TESTED...
"...YES!"

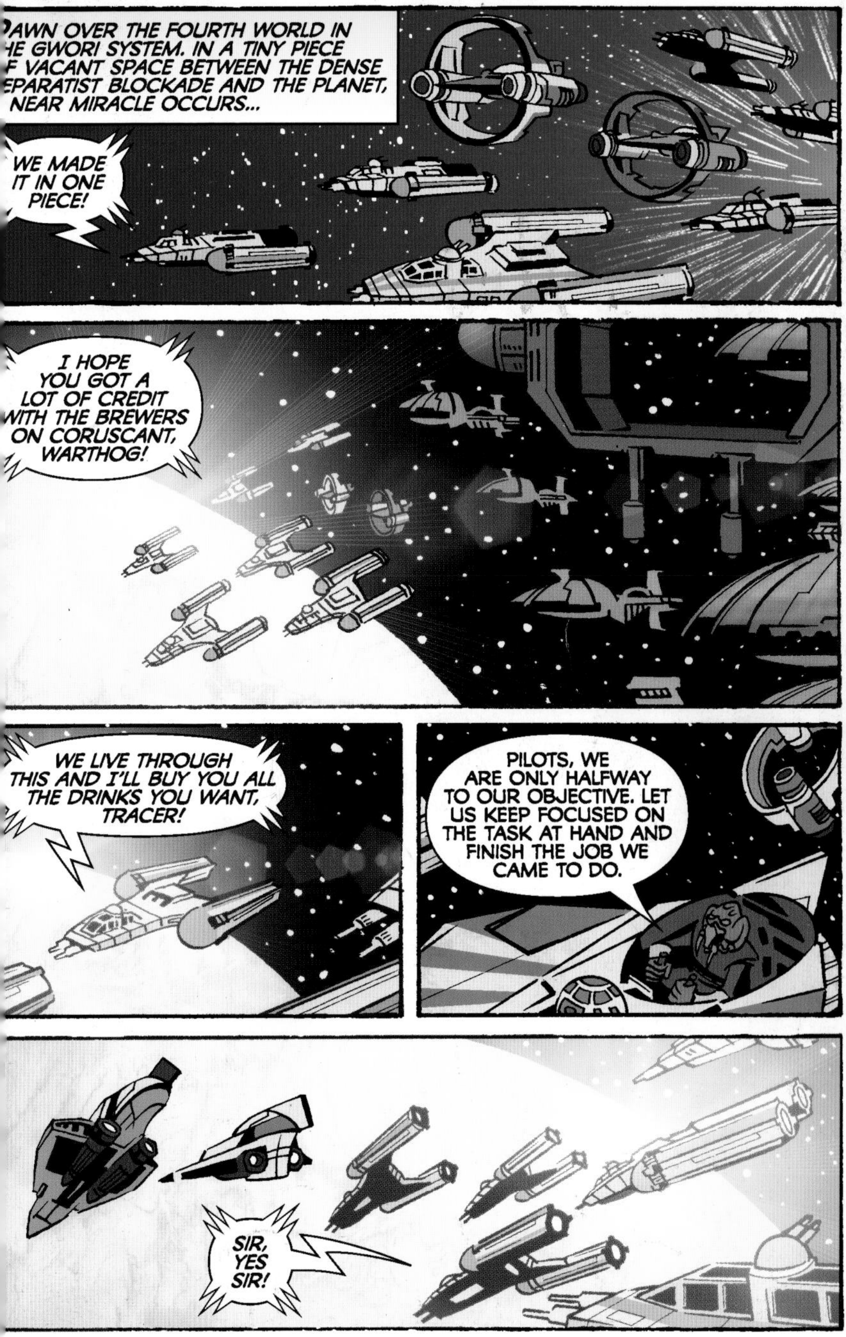
AWN OVER THE FOURTH WORLD IN
IE GWORI SYSTEM. IN A TINY PIECE
F VACANT SPACE BETWEEN THE DENSE
EPARATIST BLOCKADE AND THE PLANET,
NEAR MIRACLE OCCURS...
WE MADE IT IN ONE PIECE!
I HOPE YOU GOT A LOT OF CREDIT WITH THE BREWERS ON CORUSCANT, WARTHOG!
WE LIVE THROUGH THIS AND I'LL BUY YOU ALL THE DRINKS YOU WANT, TRACER!
PILOTS, WE ARE ONLY HALFWAY TO OUR OBJECTIVE. LET US KEEP FOCUSED ON THE TASK AT HAND AND FINISH THE JOB WE CAME TO DO.
SIR, YES SIR!

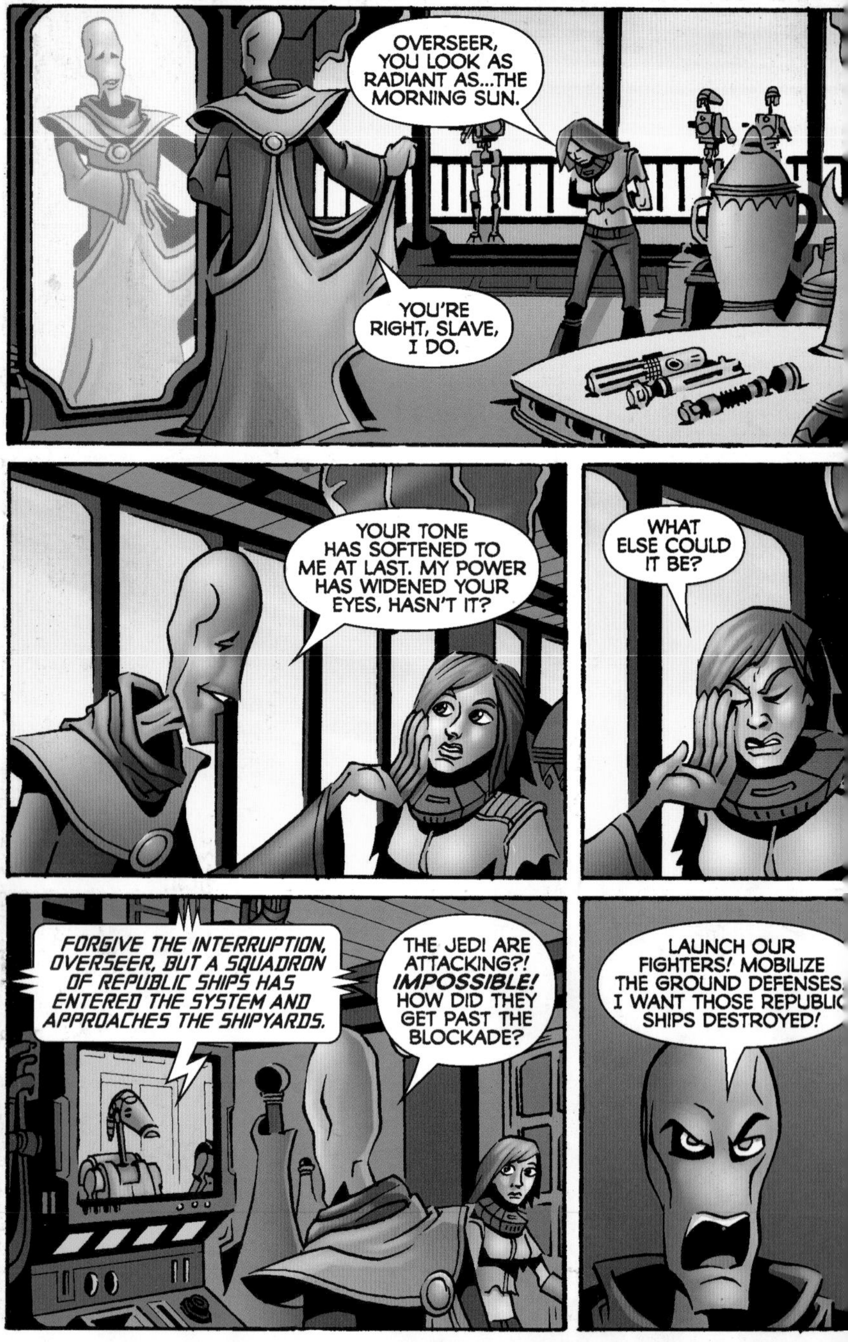
OVERSEER, YOU LOOK AS RADIANT AS...THE MORNING SUN.
YOU'RE RIGHT, SLAVE, I DO.
YOUR TONE HAS SOFTENED TO ME AT LAST. MY POWER HAS WIDENED YOUR EYES, HASN'T IT?
WHAT ELSE COULD IT BE?
FORGIVE THE INTERRUPTION, OVERSEER, BUT A SQUADRON OF REPUBLIC SHIPS HAS ENTERED THE SYSTEM AND APPROACHES THE SHIPYARDS.
THE JEDI ARE ATTACKING?! IMPOSSIBLE! HOW DID THEY GET PAST THE BLOCKADE?
LAUNCH OUR FIGHTERS! MOBILIZE THE GROUND DEFENSES. I WANT THOSE REPUBLIC SHIPS DESTROYED!

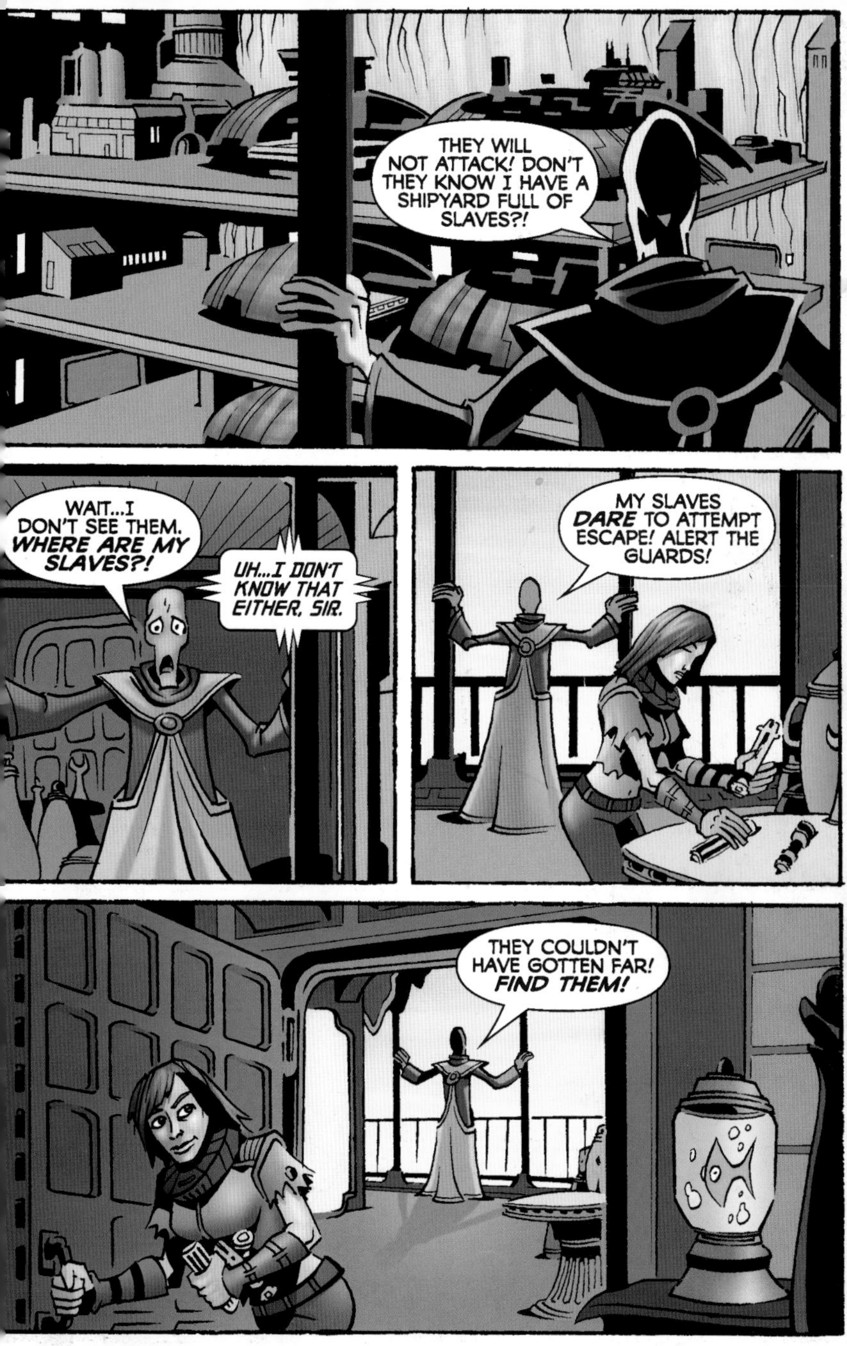
THEY WILL NOT ATTACK! DON'T THEY KNOW I HAVE A SHIPYARD FULL OF SLAVES?!
WAIT...I DON'T SEE THEM. WHERE ARE MY SLAVES?!
UH...I DON'T KNOW THAT EITHER, SIR.
MY SLAVES DARE TO ATTEMPT ESCAPE! ALERT THE GUARDS!
THEY COULDN'T HAVE GOTTEN FAR! FIND THEM!

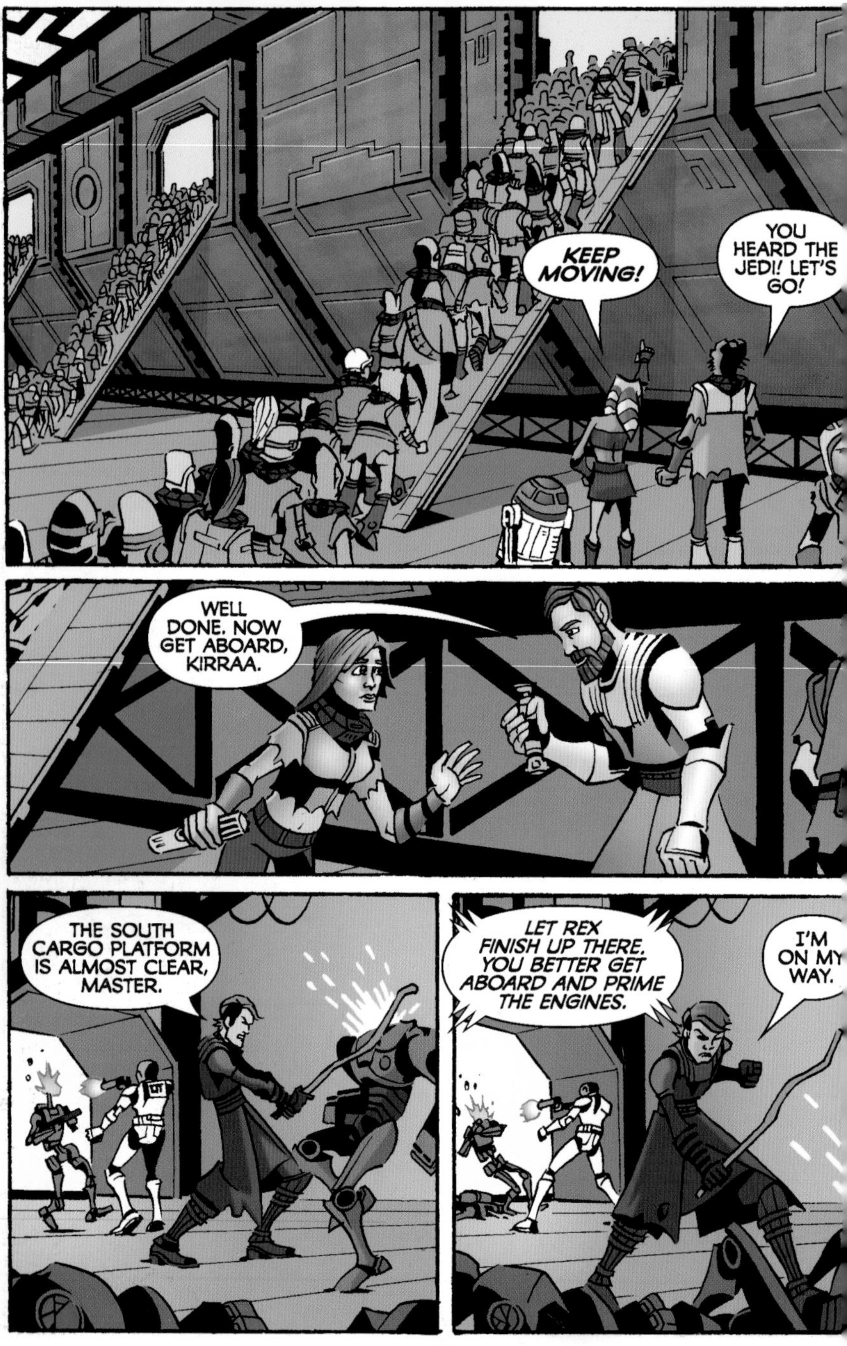
KEEP MOVING!
YOU HEARD THE JEDI! LET'S GO!
WELL DONE. NOW GET ABOARD, KIRRAA.
THE SOUTH CARGO PLATFORM IS ALMOST CLEAR, MASTER.
LET REX FINISH UP THERE. YOU BETTER GET ABOARD AND PRIME THE ENGINES.
I'M ON MY WAY.

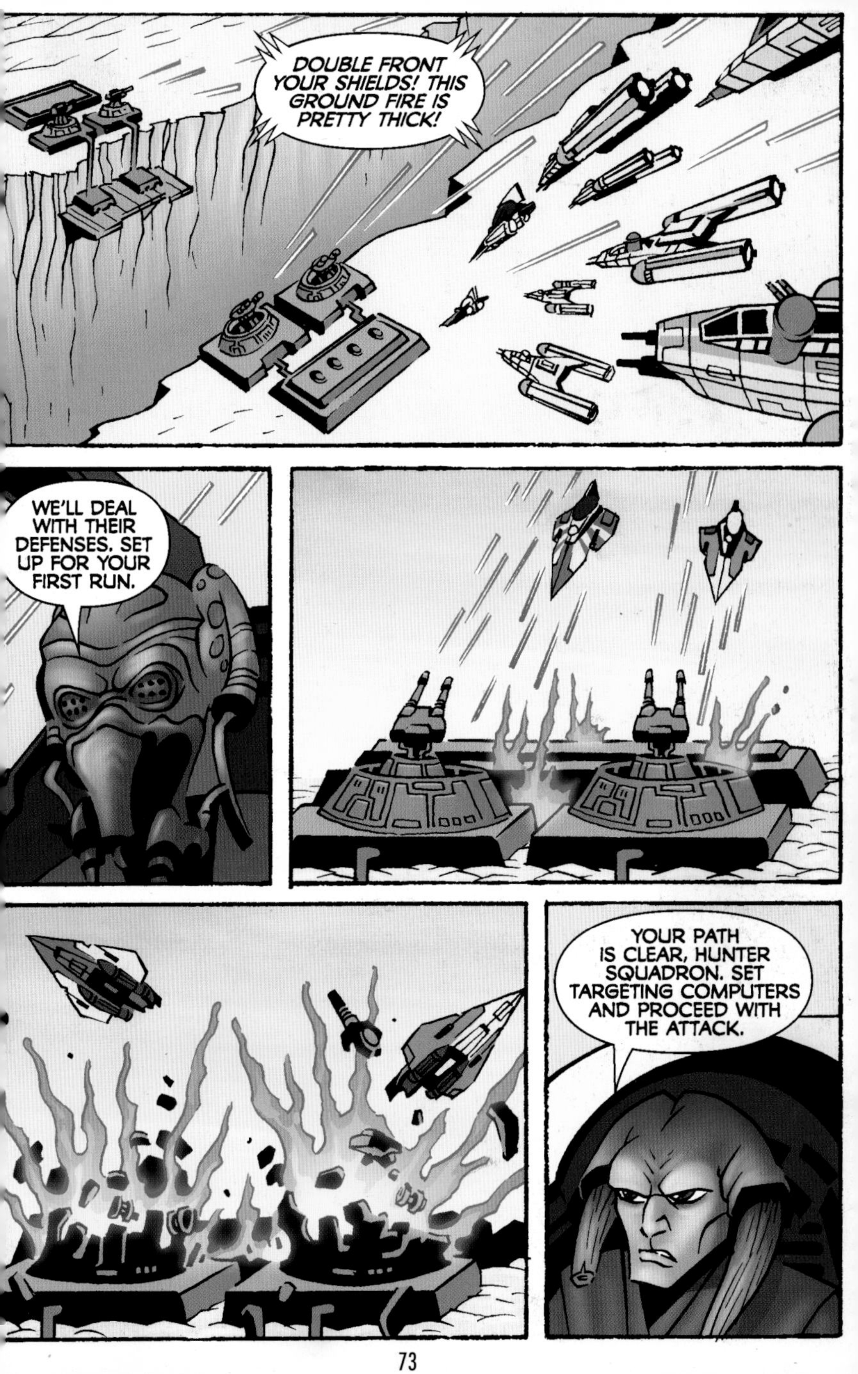
DOUBLE FRONT YOUR SHIELDS! THIS GROUND FIRE IS PRETTY THICK!
WE'LL DEAL WITH THEIR DEFENSES. SET UP FOR YOUR FIRST RUN.
YOUR PATH IS CLEAR, HUNTER SQUADRON. SET TARGETING COMPUTERS AND PROCEED WITH THE ATTACK.

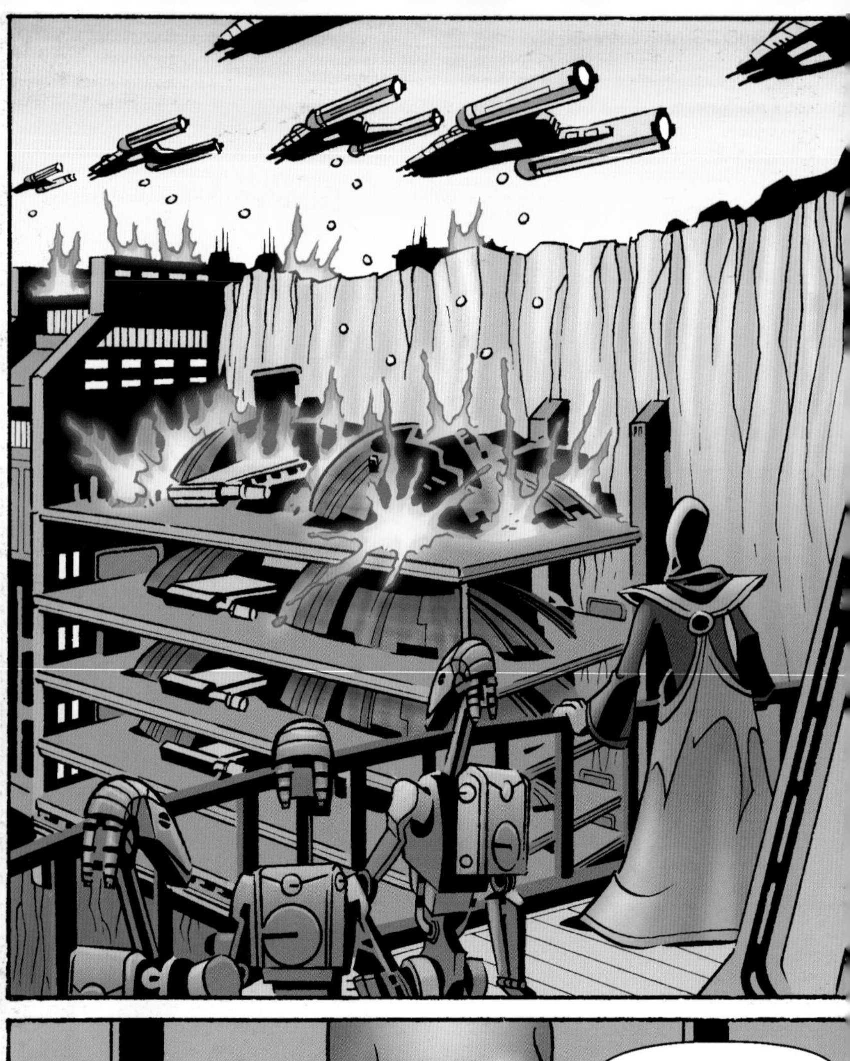

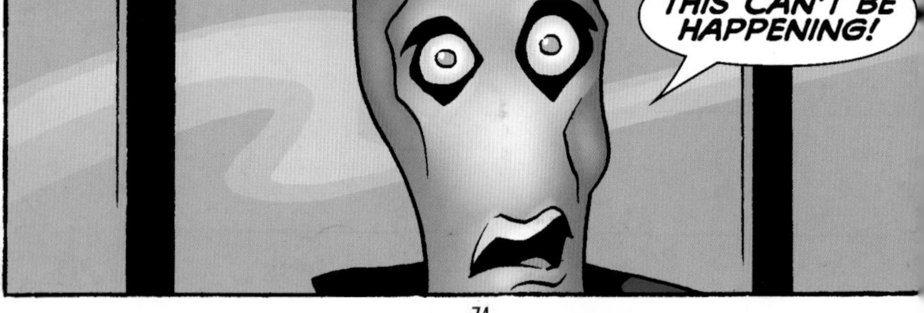
THIS CAN'T BE HAPPENING!

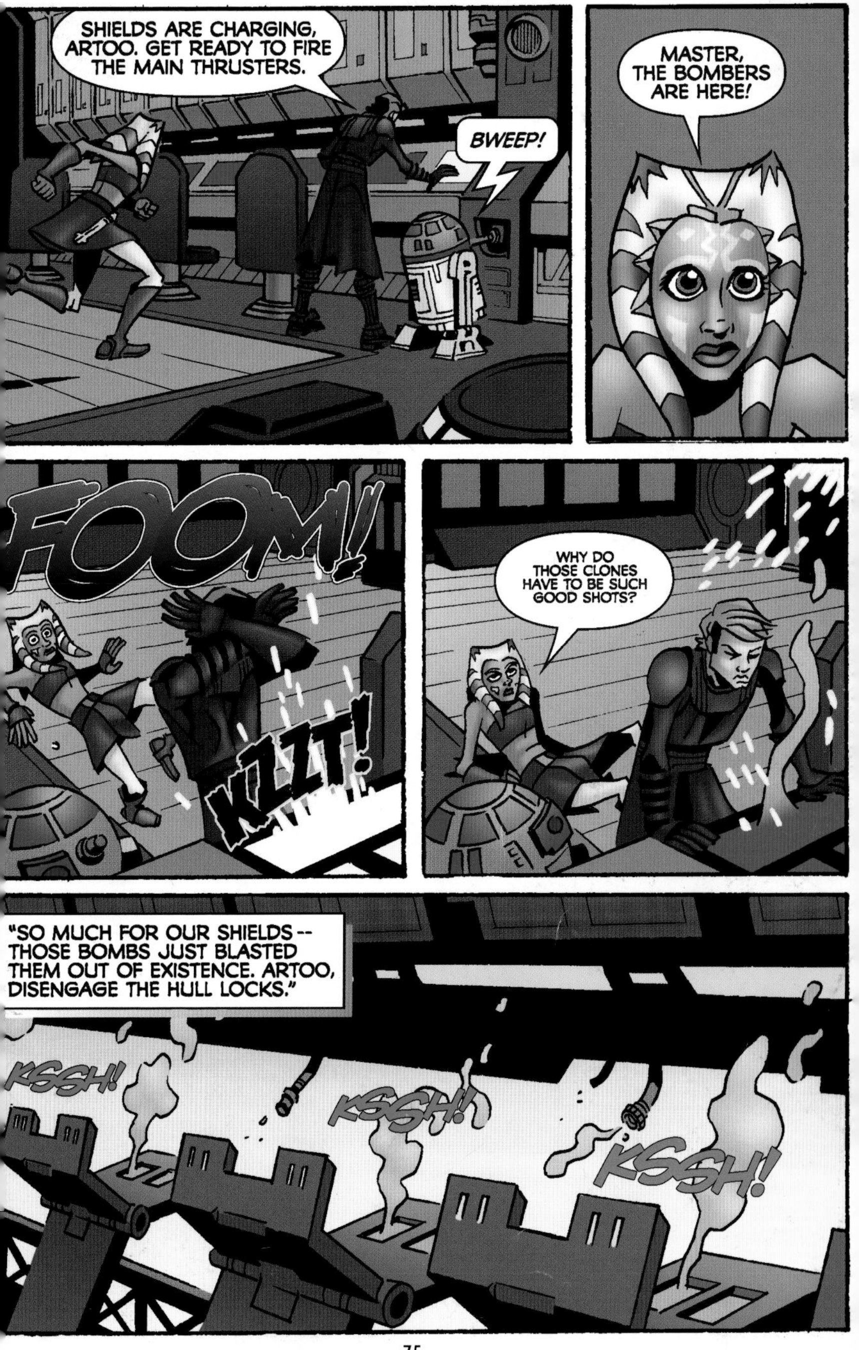
SHIELDS ARE CHARGING, ARTOO. GET READY TO FIRE THE MAIN THRUSTERS.
BWEEP!
MASTER, THE BOMBERS ARE HERE!
FOOM!!
KZZT!
WHY DO THOSE CLONES HAVE TO BE SUCH GOOD SHOTS?
"SO MUCH FOR OUR SHIELDS -- THOSE BOMBS JUST BLASTED THEM OUT OF EXISTENCE. ARTOO, DISENGAGE THE HULL LOCKS."
KSSH!
KSSH!
KSSH!

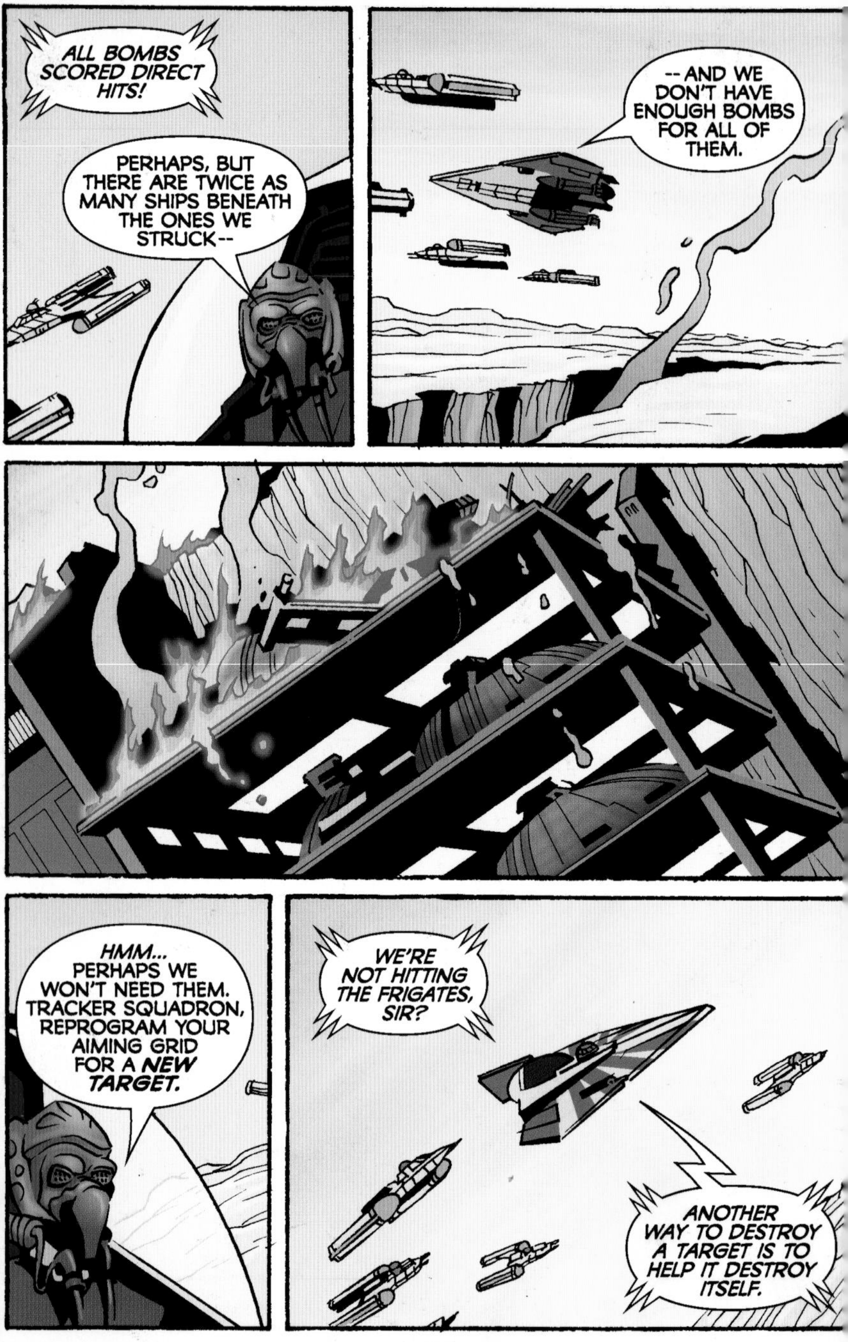
ALL BOMBS SCORED DIRECT HITS!
PERHAPS, BUT THERE ARE TWICE AS MANY SHIPS BENEATH THE ONES WE STRUCK--
-- AND WE DON'T HAVE ENOUGH BOMBS FOR ALL OF THEM.
HMM... PERHAPS WE WON'T NEED THEM. TRACKER SQUADRON, REPROGRAM YOUR AIMING GRID FOR A *NEW TARGET.*
WE'RE NOT HITTING THE FRIGATES, SIR?
ANOTHER WAY TO DESTROY A TARGET IS TO HELP IT DESTROY ITSELF.

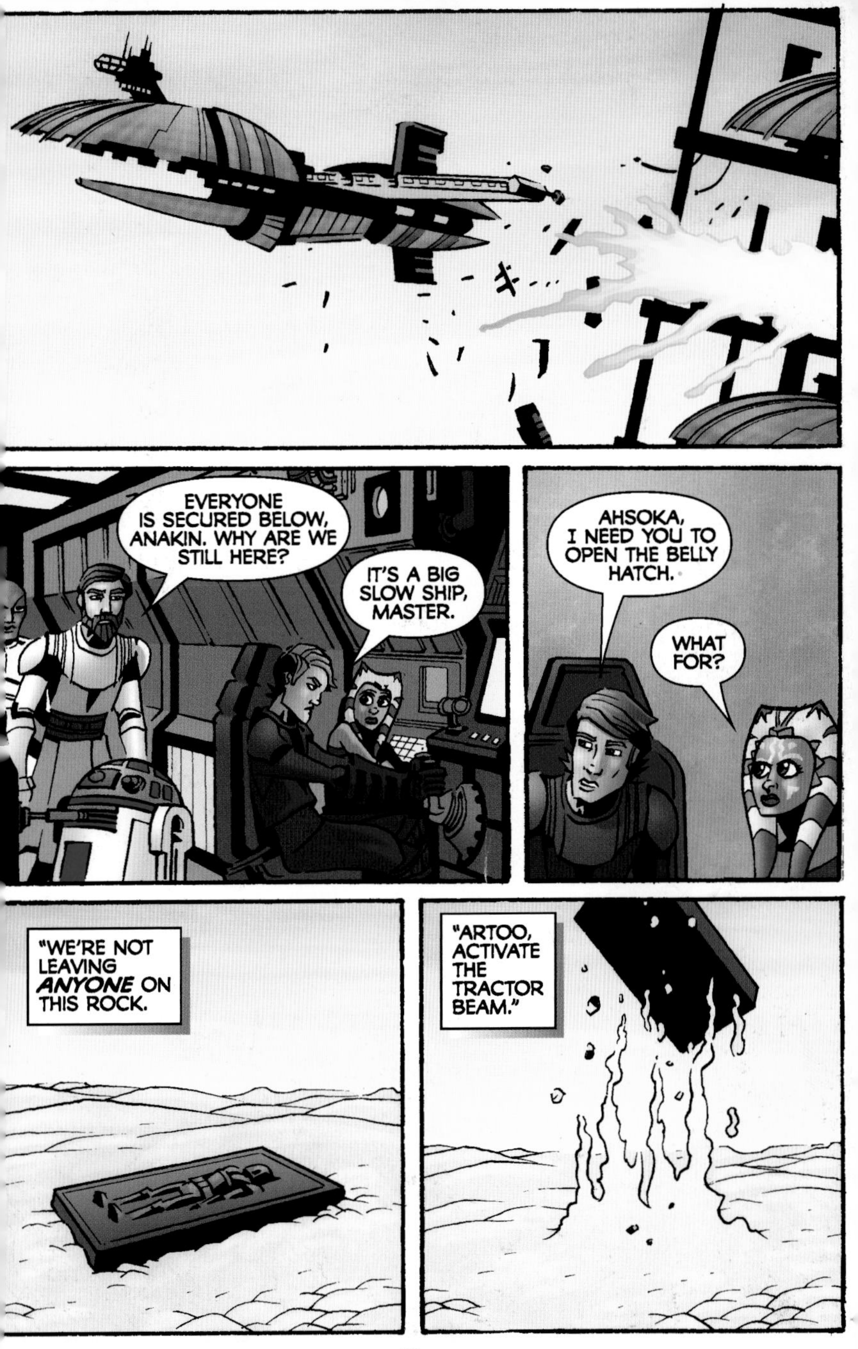
EVERYONE IS SECURED BELOW, ANAKIN. WHY ARE WE STILL HERE?
IT'S A BIG SLOW SHIP, MASTER.
AHSOKA, I NEED YOU TO OPEN THE BELLY HATCH.
WHAT FOR?
"WE'RE NOT LEAVING *ANYONE* ON THIS ROCK.
"ARTOO, ACTIVATE THE TRACTOR BEAM."

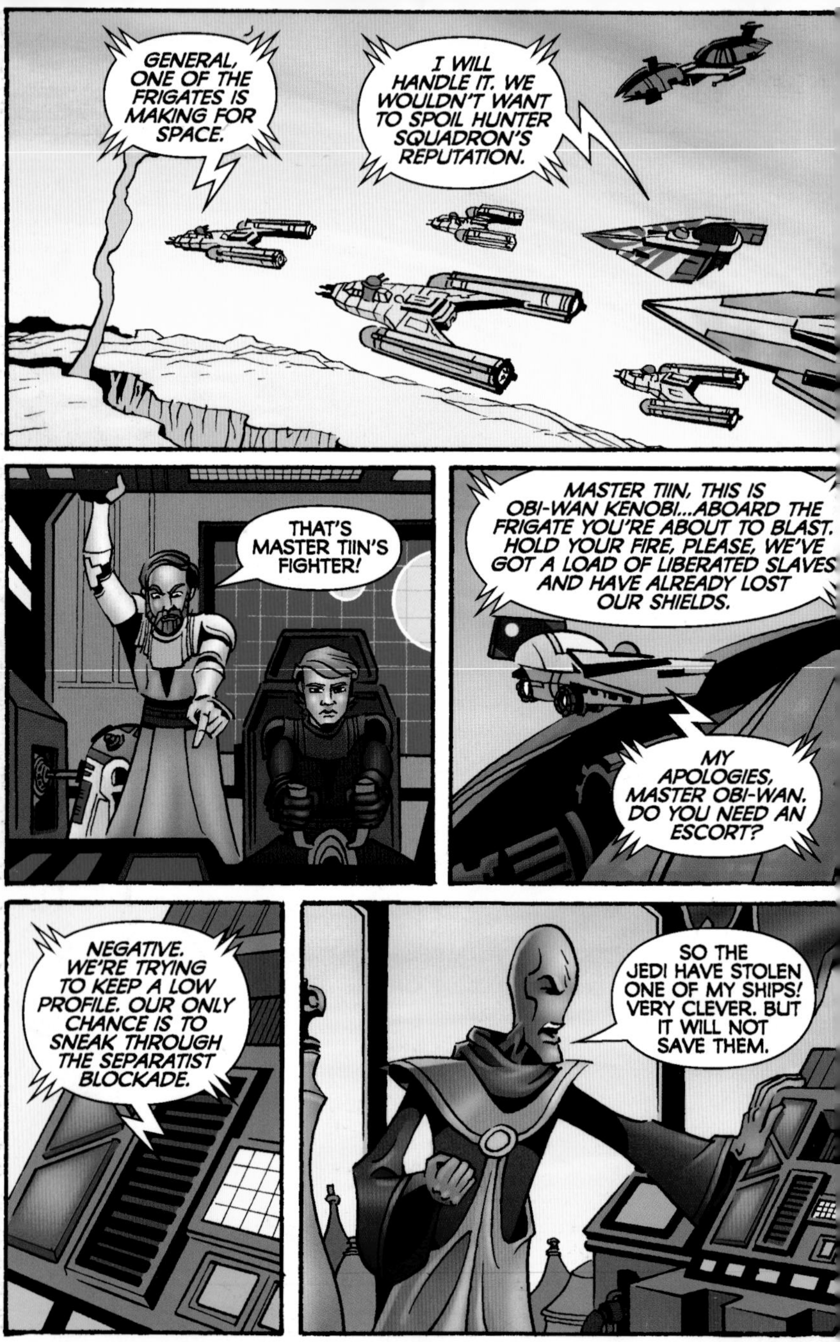
GENERAL, ONE OF THE FRIGATES IS MAKING FOR SPACE.
I WILL HANDLE IT. WE WOULDN'T WANT TO SPOIL HUNTER SQUADRON'S REPUTATION.
THAT'S MASTER TIIN'S FIGHTER!
MASTER TIIN, THIS IS OBI-WAN KENOBI...ABOARD THE FRIGATE YOU'RE ABOUT TO BLAST. HOLD YOUR FIRE, PLEASE, WE'VE GOT A LOAD OF LIBERATED SLAVES AND HAVE ALREADY LOST OUR SHIELDS.
MY APOLOGIES, MASTER OBI-WAN. DO YOU NEED AN ESCORT?
NEGATIVE. WE'RE TRYING TO KEEP A LOW PROFILE. OUR ONLY CHANCE IS TO SNEAK THROUGH THE SEPARATIST BLOCKADE.
SO THE JEDI HAVE STOLEN ONE OF MY SHIPS! VERY CLEVER. BUT IT WILL NOT SAVE THEM.

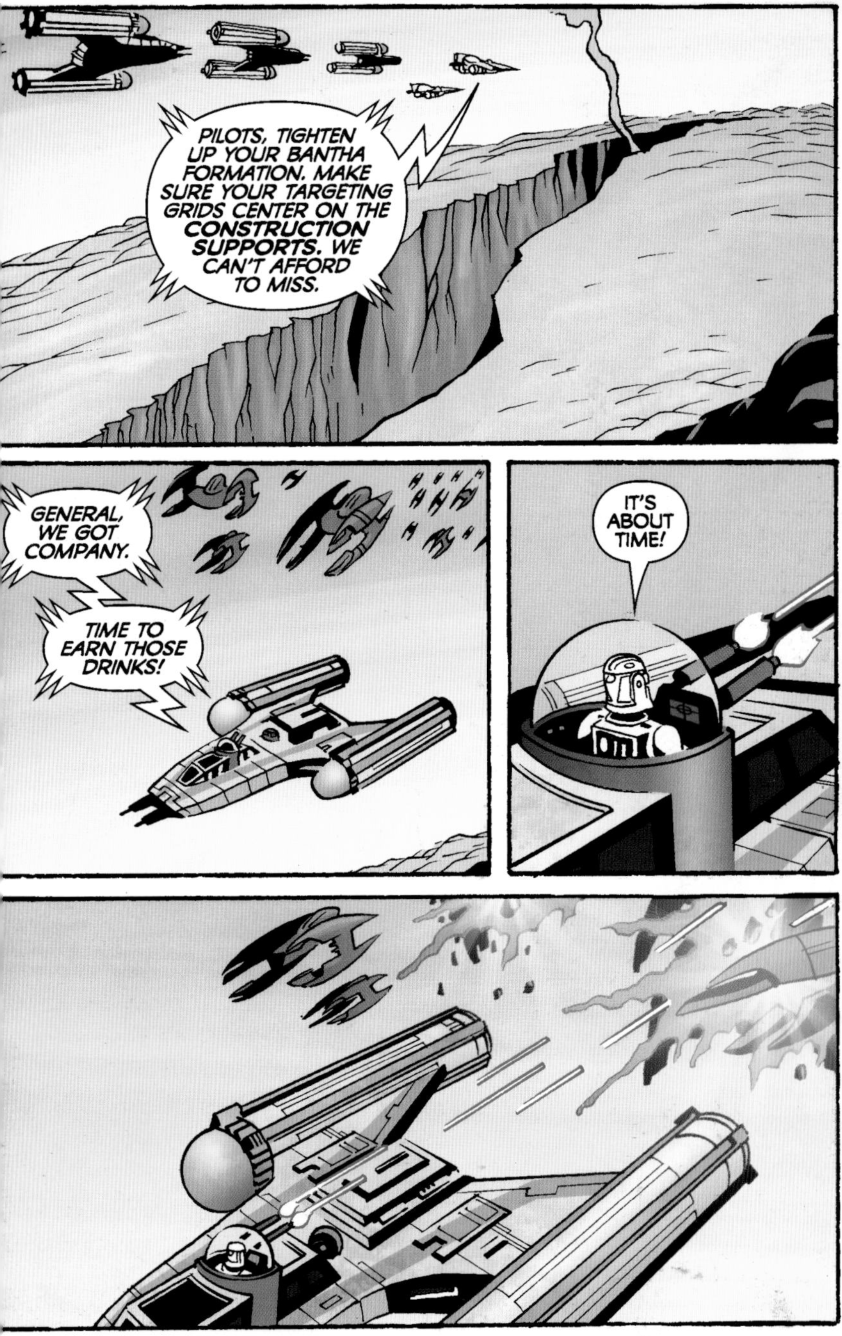
PILOTS, TIGHTEN UP YOUR BANTHA FORMATION. MAKE SURE YOUR TARGETING GRIDS CENTER ON THE CONSTRUCTION SUPPORTS. WE CAN'T AFFORD TO MISS.
GENERAL, WE GOT COMPANY.
TIME TO EARN THOSE DRINKS!
IT'S ABOUT TIME!

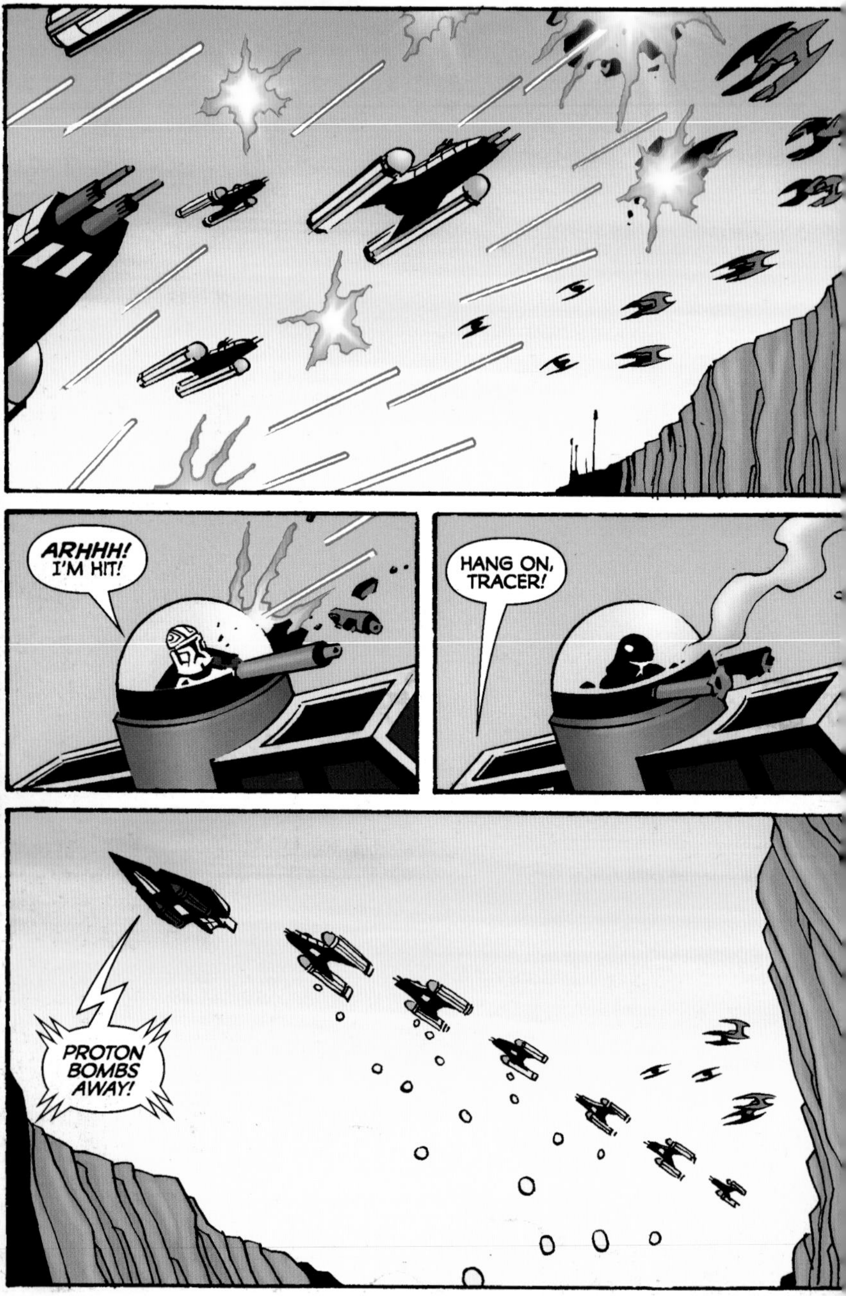
ARHHH! I'M HIT!
HANG ON, TRACER!
PROTON BOMBS AWAY!

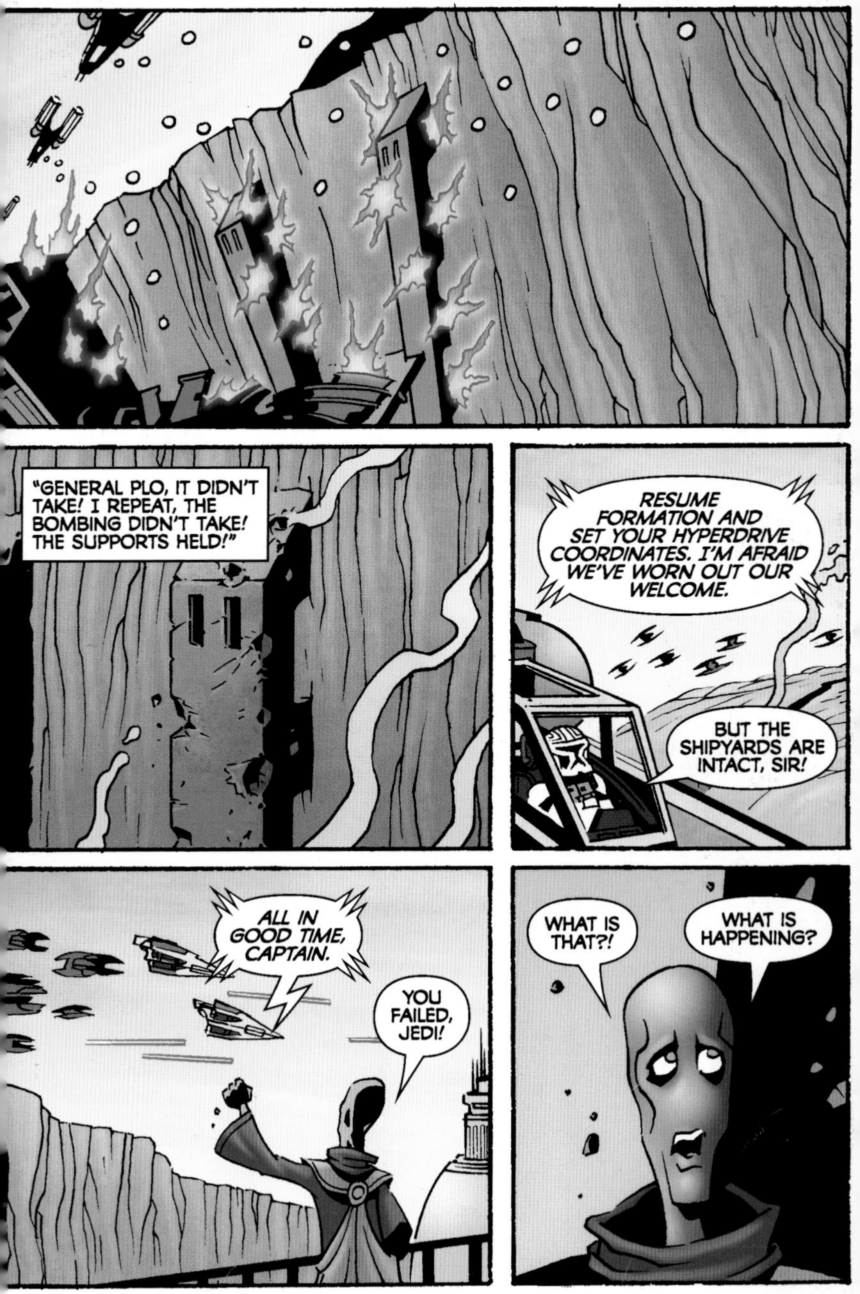
"GENERAL PLO, IT DIDN'T TAKE! I REPEAT, THE BOMBING DIDN'T TAKE! THE SUPPORTS HELD!"
RESUME FORMATION AND SET YOUR HYPERDRIVE COORDINATES. I'M AFRAID WE'VE WORN OUT OUR WELCOME.
BUT THE SHIPYARDS ARE INTACT, SIR!
ALL IN GOOD TIME, CAPTAIN.
YOU FAILED, JEDI!
WHAT IS THAT?!
WHAT IS HAPPENING?

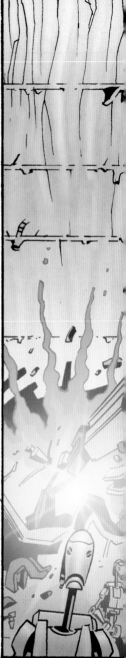

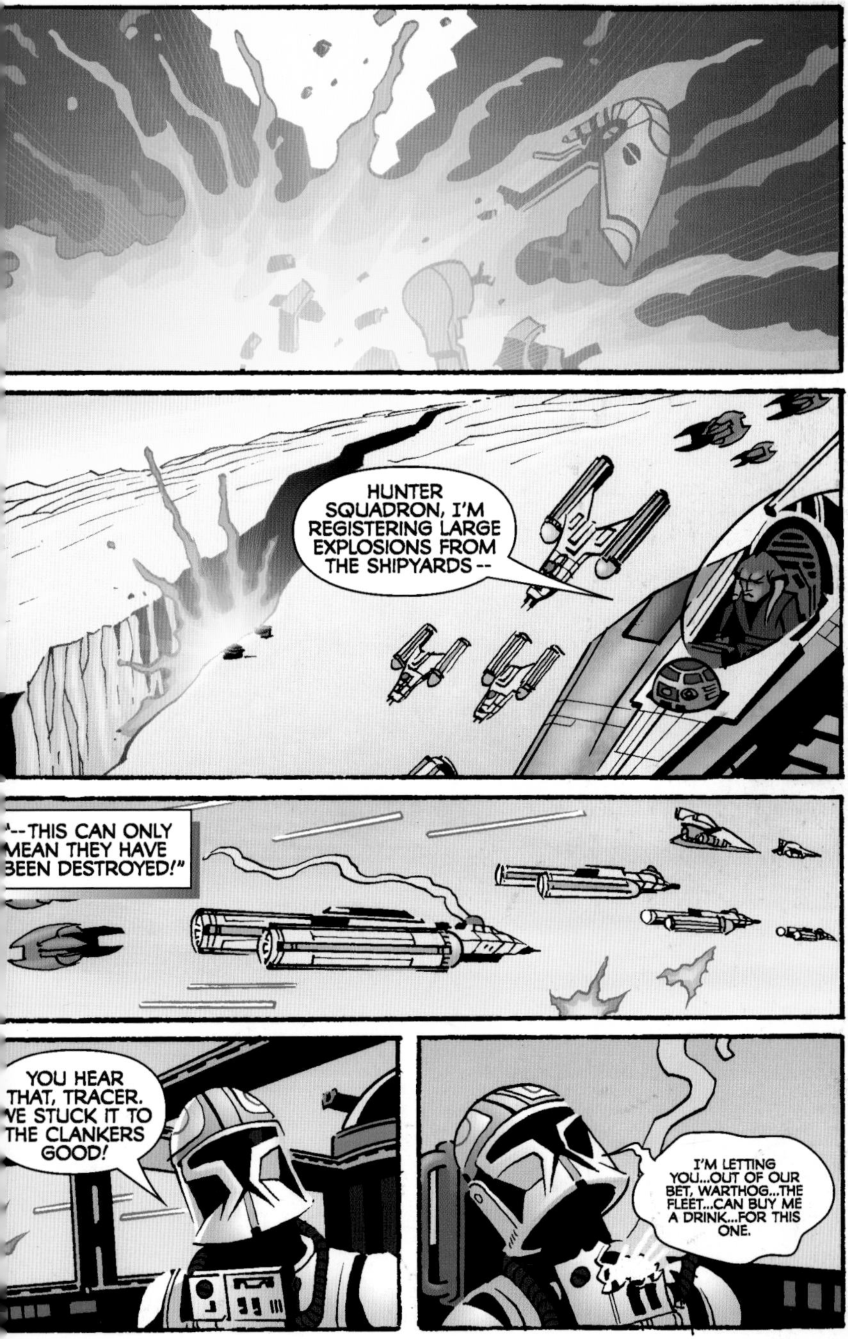
HUNTER SQUADRON, I'M REGISTERING LARGE EXPLOSIONS FROM THE SHIPYARDS --
"--THIS CAN ONLY MEAN THEY HAVE BEEN DESTROYED!"
YOU HEAR THAT, TRACER. VE STUCK IT TO THE CLANKERS GOOD!
I'M LETTING YOU...OUT OF OUR BET, WARTHOG...THE FLEET...CAN BUY ME A DRINK...FOR THIS ONE.

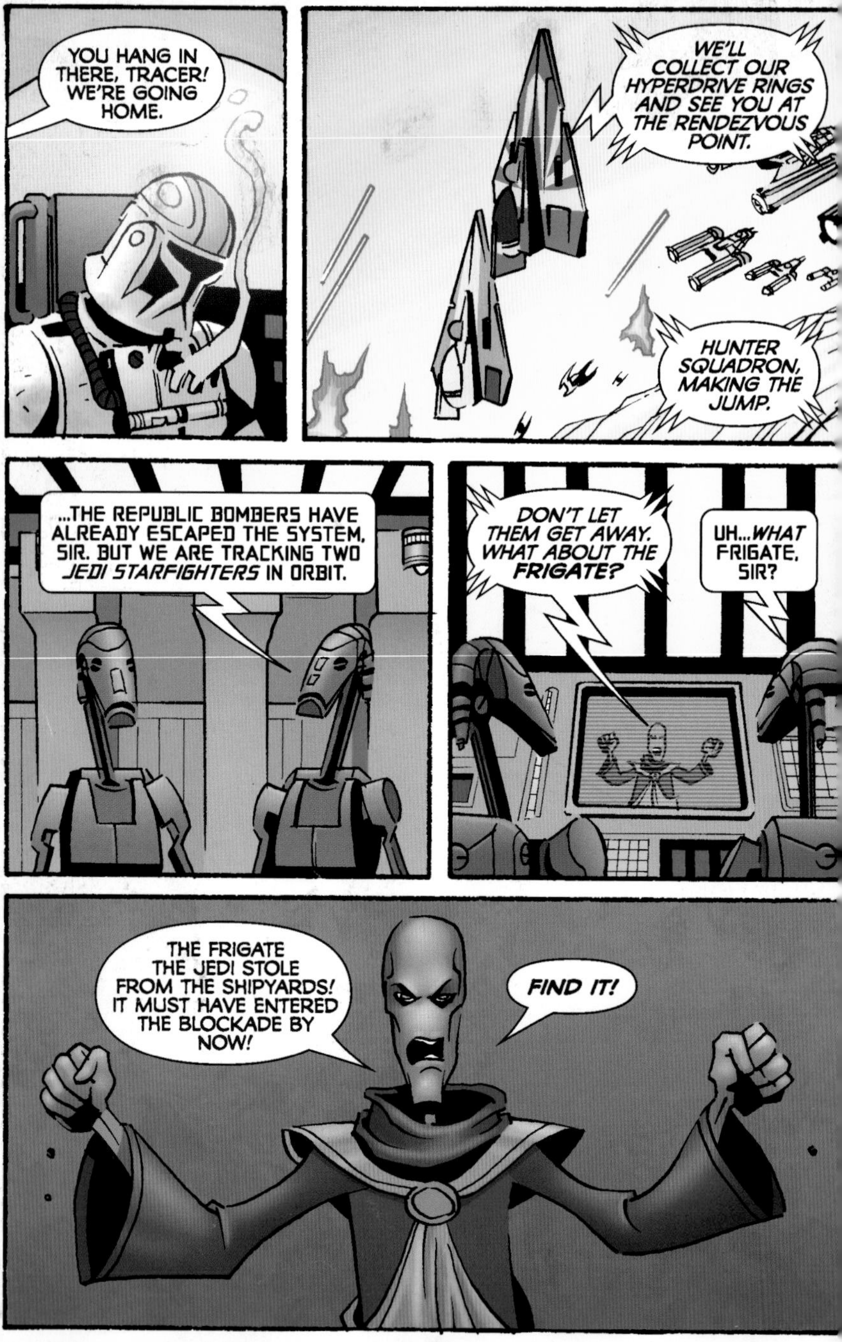
YOU HANG IN THERE, TRACER! WE'RE GOING HOME.
WE'LL COLLECT OUR HYPERDRIVE RINGS AND SEE YOU AT THE RENDEZVOUS POINT.
HUNTER SQUADRON, MAKING THE JUMP.
...THE REPUBLIC BOMBERS HAVE ALREADY ESCAPED THE SYSTEM, SIR. BUT WE ARE TRACKING TWO *JEDI STARFIGHTERS* IN ORBIT.
DON'T LET THEM GET AWAY. WHAT ABOUT THE **FRIGATE?**
UH...*WHAT* FRIGATE, SIR?
THE FRIGATE THE JEDI STOLE FROM THE SHIPYARDS! IT MUST HAVE ENTERED THE BLOCKADE BY NOW!
FIND IT!

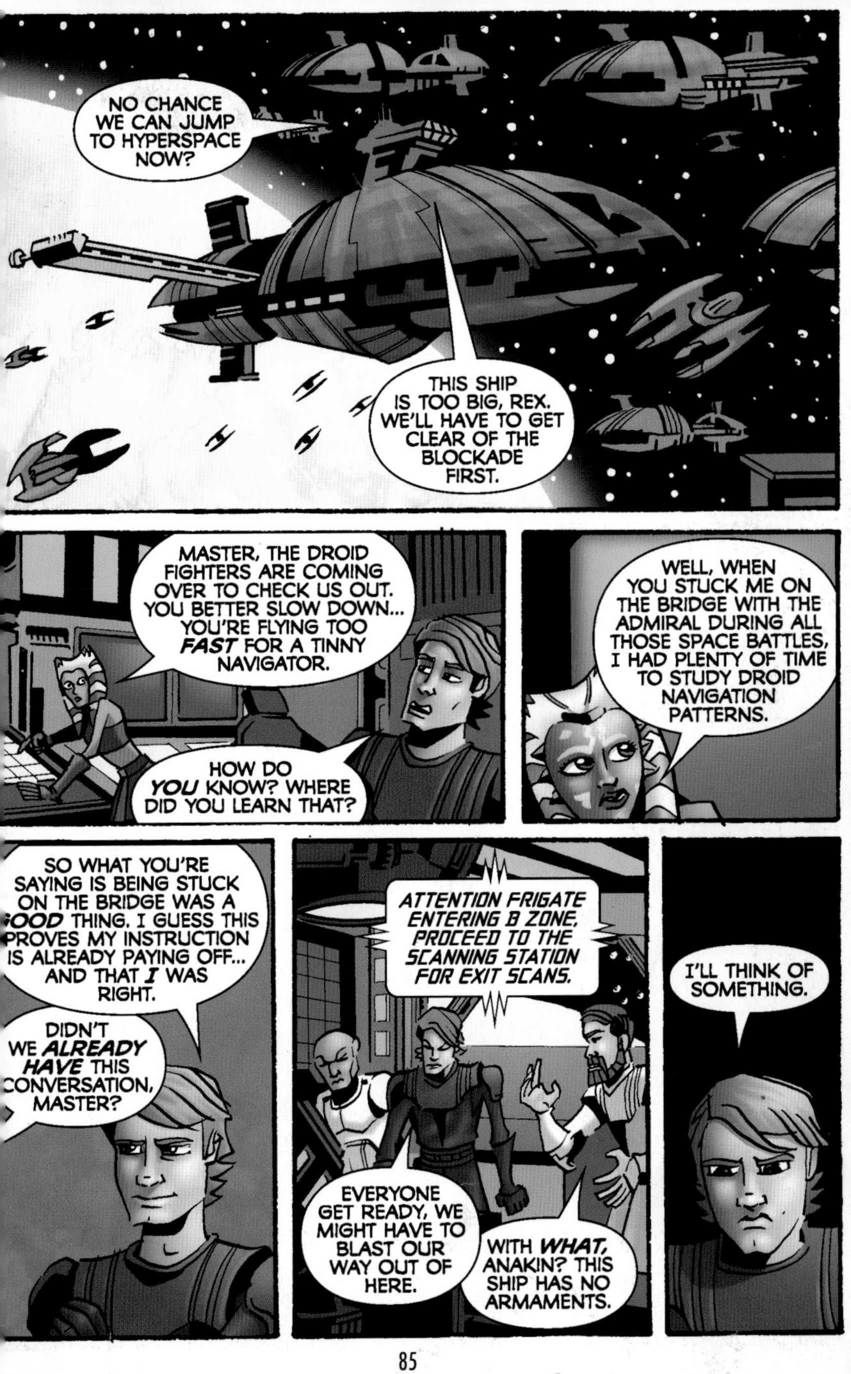
NO CHANCE WE CAN JUMP TO HYPERSPACE NOW?
THIS SHIP IS TOO BIG, REX. WE'LL HAVE TO GET CLEAR OF THE BLOCKADE FIRST.
MASTER, THE DROID FIGHTERS ARE COMING OVER TO CHECK US OUT. YOU BETTER SLOW DOWN... YOU'RE FLYING TOO *FAST* FOR A TINNY NAVIGATOR.
HOW DO *YOU* KNOW? WHERE DID YOU LEARN THAT?
WELL, WHEN YOU STUCK ME ON THE BRIDGE WITH THE ADMIRAL DURING ALL THOSE SPACE BATTLES, I HAD PLENTY OF TIME TO STUDY DROID NAVIGATION PATTERNS.
SO WHAT YOU'RE SAYING IS BEING STUCK ON THE BRIDGE WAS A *GOOD* THING. I GUESS THIS PROVES MY INSTRUCTION IS ALREADY PAYING OFF... AND THAT *I* WAS RIGHT.
DIDN'T WE *ALREADY HAVE* THIS CONVERSATION, MASTER?
ATTENTION FRIGATE ENTERING B ZONE, PROCEED TO THE SCANNING STATION FOR EXIT SCANS.
EVERYONE GET READY, WE MIGHT HAVE TO BLAST OUR WAY OUT OF HERE.
WITH *WHAT,* ANAKIN? THIS SHIP HAS NO ARMAMENTS.
I'LL THINK OF SOMETHING.

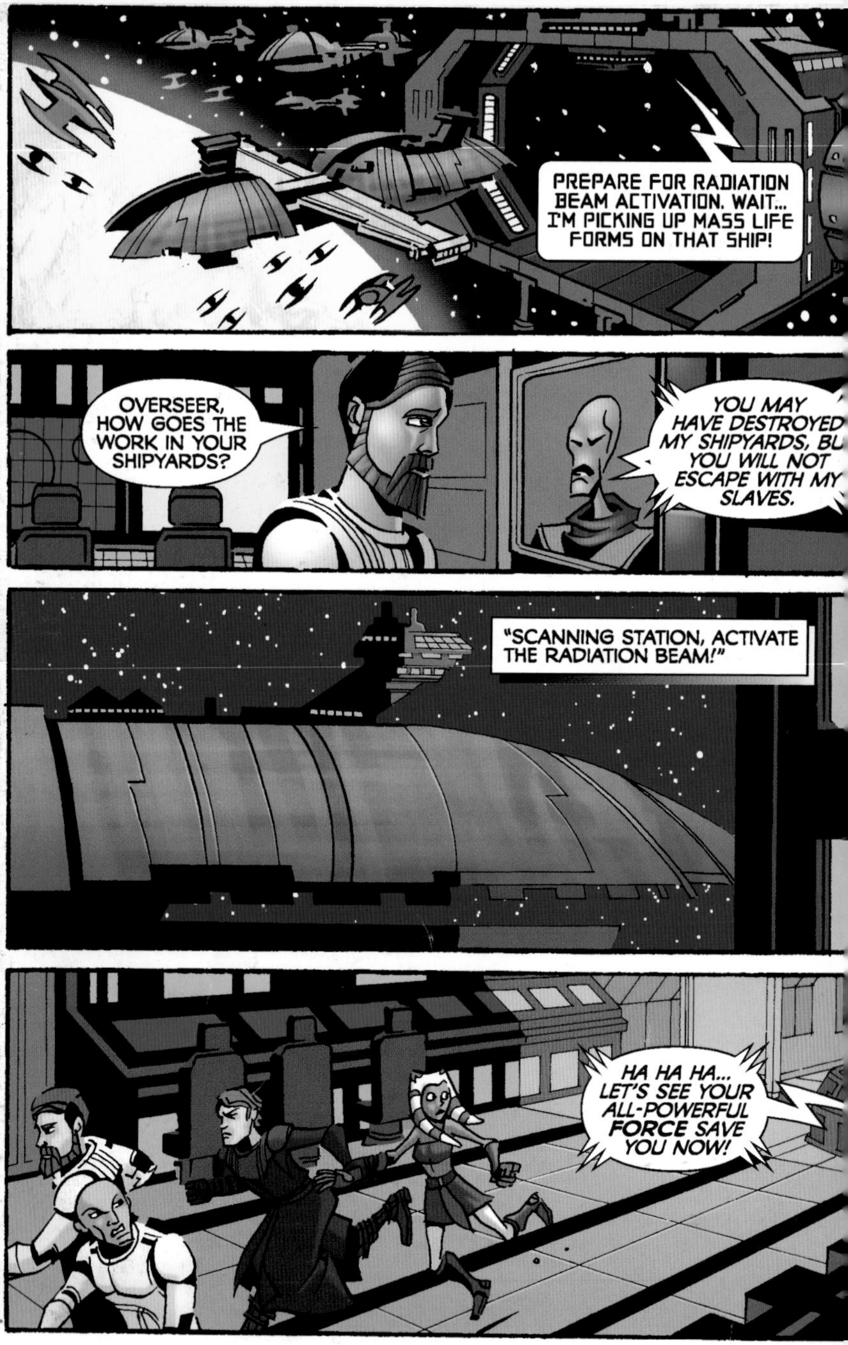
PREPARE FOR RADIATION BEAM ACTIVATION. WAIT... I'M PICKING UP MASS LIFE FORMS ON THAT SHIP!
OVERSEER, HOW GOES THE WORK IN YOUR SHIPYARDS?
YOU MAY HAVE DESTROYED MY SHIPYARDS, BU YOU WILL NOT ESCAPE WITH MY SLAVES.
"SCANNING STATION, ACTIVATE THE RADIATION BEAM!"
HA HA HA... LET'S SEE YOUR ALL-POWERFUL FORCE SAVE YOU NOW!

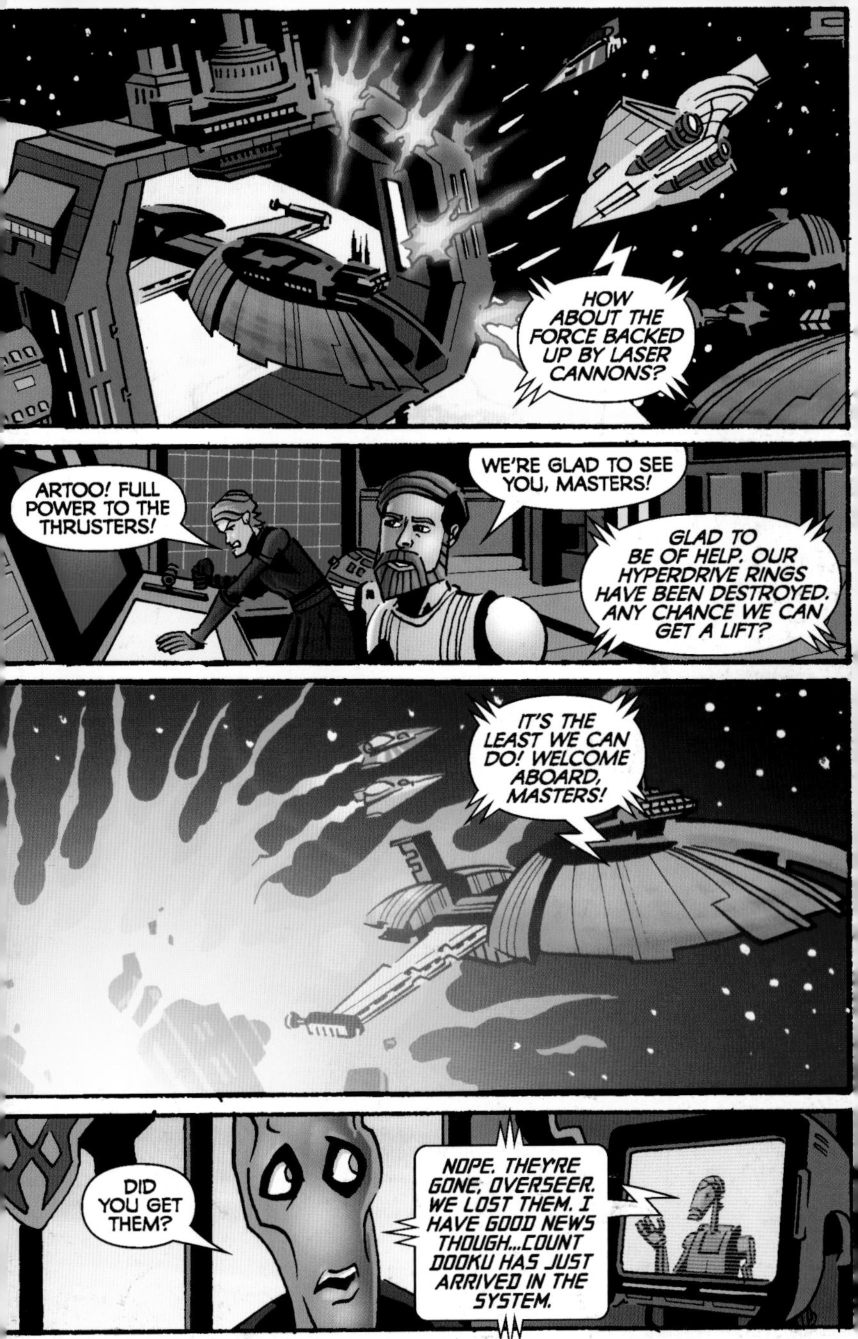
HOW ABOUT THE FORCE BACKED UP BY LASER CANNONS?
ARTOO! FULL POWER TO THE THRUSTERS!
WE'RE GLAD TO SEE YOU, MASTERS!
GLAD TO BE OF HELP. OUR HYPERDRIVE RINGS HAVE BEEN DESTROYED. ANY CHANCE WE CAN GET A LIFT?
IT'S THE LEAST WE CAN DO! WELCOME ABOARD, MASTERS!
DID YOU GET THEM?
NOPE. THEY'RE GONE, OVERSEER. WE LOST THEM. I HAVE GOOD NEWS THOUGH...COUNT DOOKU HAS JUST ARRIVED IN THE SYSTEM.

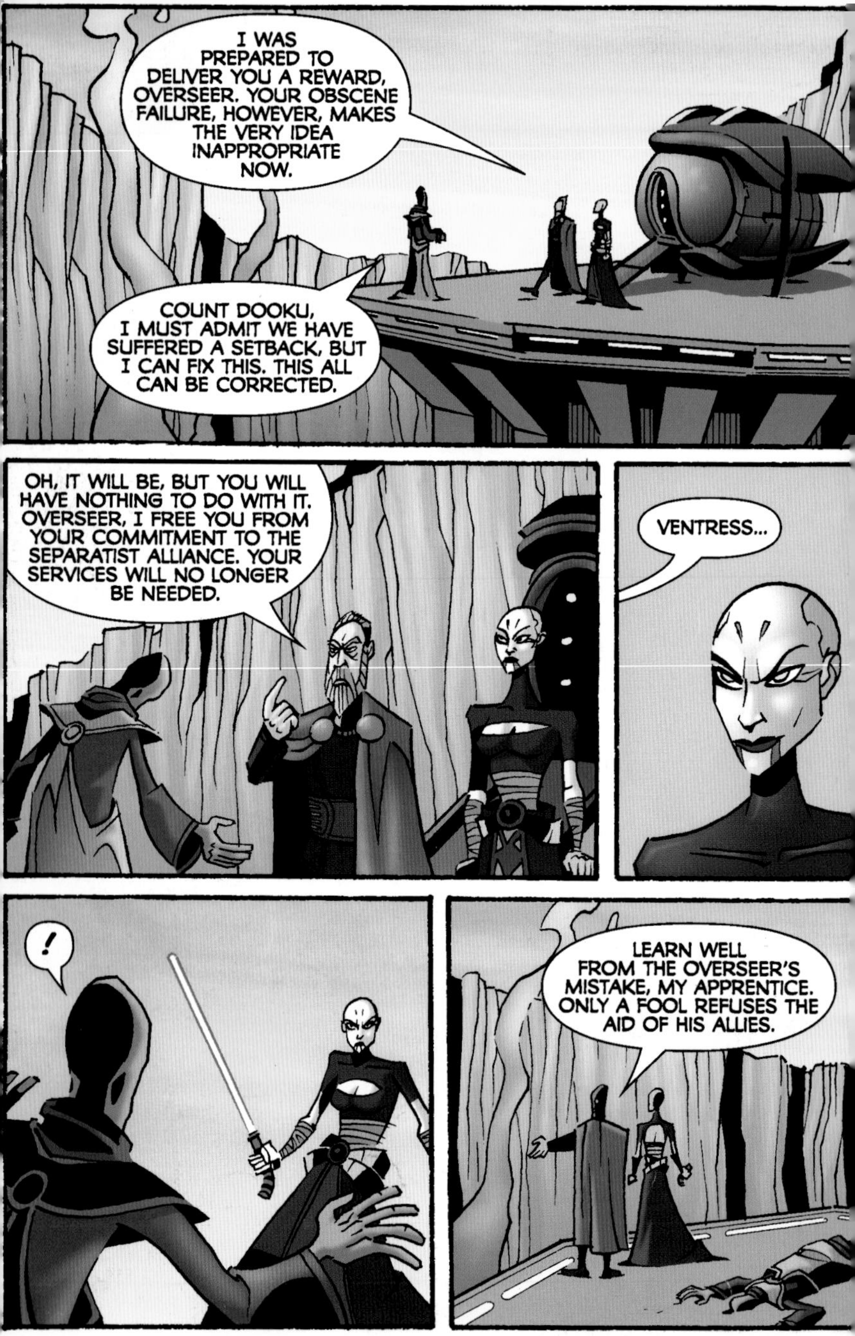
I WAS PREPARED TO DELIVER YOU A REWARD, OVERSEER. YOUR OBSCENE FAILURE, HOWEVER, MAKES THE VERY IDEA INAPPROPRIATE NOW.
COUNT DOOKU, I MUST ADMIT WE HAVE SUFFERED A SETBACK, BUT I CAN FIX THIS. THIS ALL CAN BE CORRECTED.
OH, IT WILL BE, BUT YOU WILL HAVE NOTHING TO DO WITH IT. OVERSEER, I FREE YOU FROM YOUR COMMITMENT TO THE SEPARATIST ALLIANCE. YOUR SERVICES WILL NO LONGER BE NEEDED.
VENTRESS...
!
LEARN WELL FROM THE OVERSEER'S MISTAKE, MY APPRENTICE. ONLY A FOOL REFUSES THE AID OF HIS ALLIES.

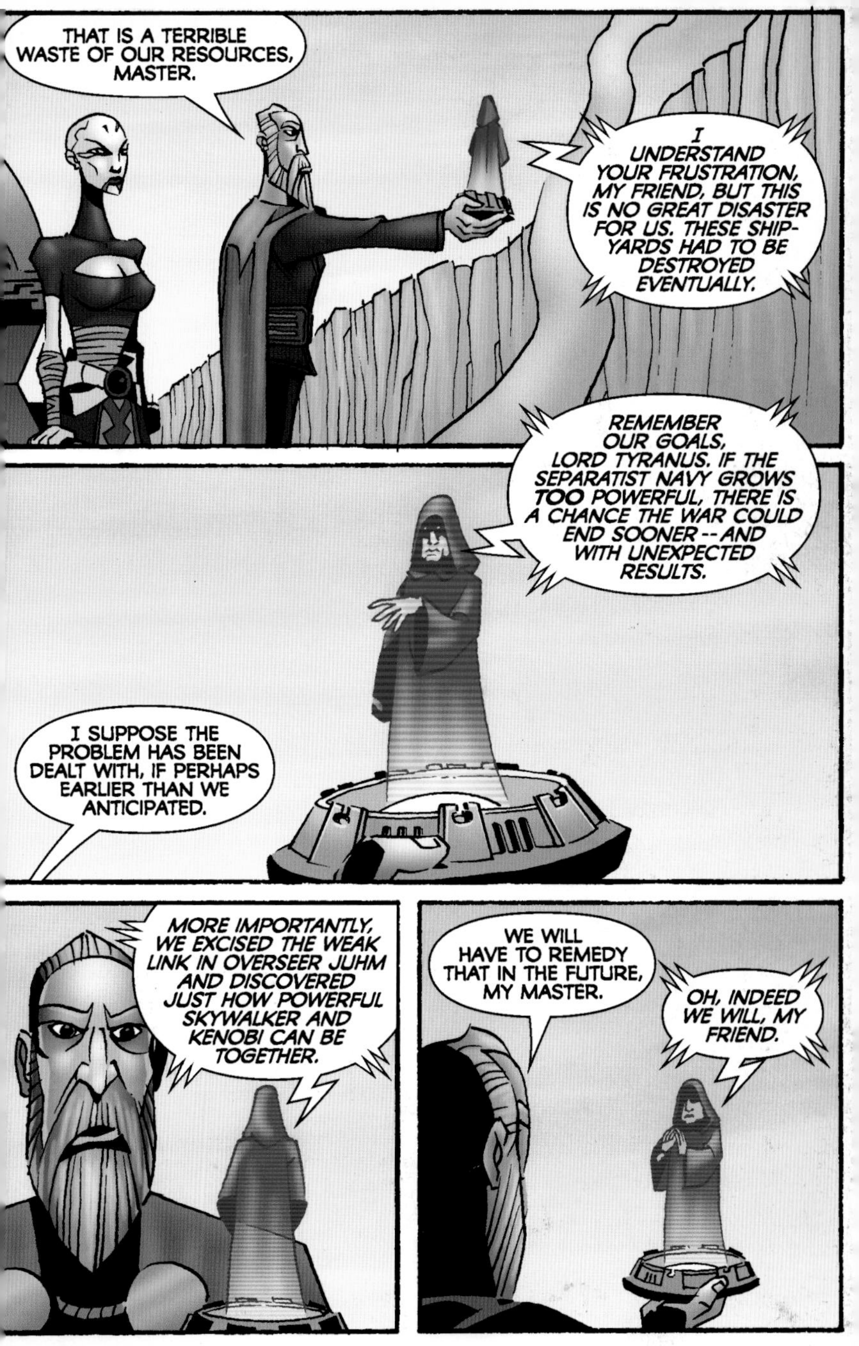
THAT IS A TERRIBLE WASTE OF OUR RESOURCES, MASTER.
I UNDERSTAND YOUR FRUSTRATION, MY FRIEND, BUT THIS IS NO GREAT DISASTER FOR US. THESE SHIP-YARDS HAD TO BE DESTROYED EVENTUALLY.
REMEMBER OUR GOALS, LORD TYRANUS. IF THE SEPARATIST NAVY GROWS TOO POWERFUL, THERE IS A CHANCE THE WAR COULD END SOONER--AND WITH UNEXPECTED RESULTS.
I SUPPOSE THE PROBLEM HAS BEEN DEALT WITH, IF PERHAPS EARLIER THAN WE ANTICIPATED.
MORE IMPORTANTLY, WE EXCISED THE WEAK LINK IN OVERSEER JUHM AND DISCOVERED JUST HOW POWERFUL SKYWALKER AND KENOBI CAN BE TOGETHER.
WE WILL HAVE TO REMEDY THAT IN THE FUTURE, MY MASTER.
OH, INDEED WE WILL, MY FRIEND.

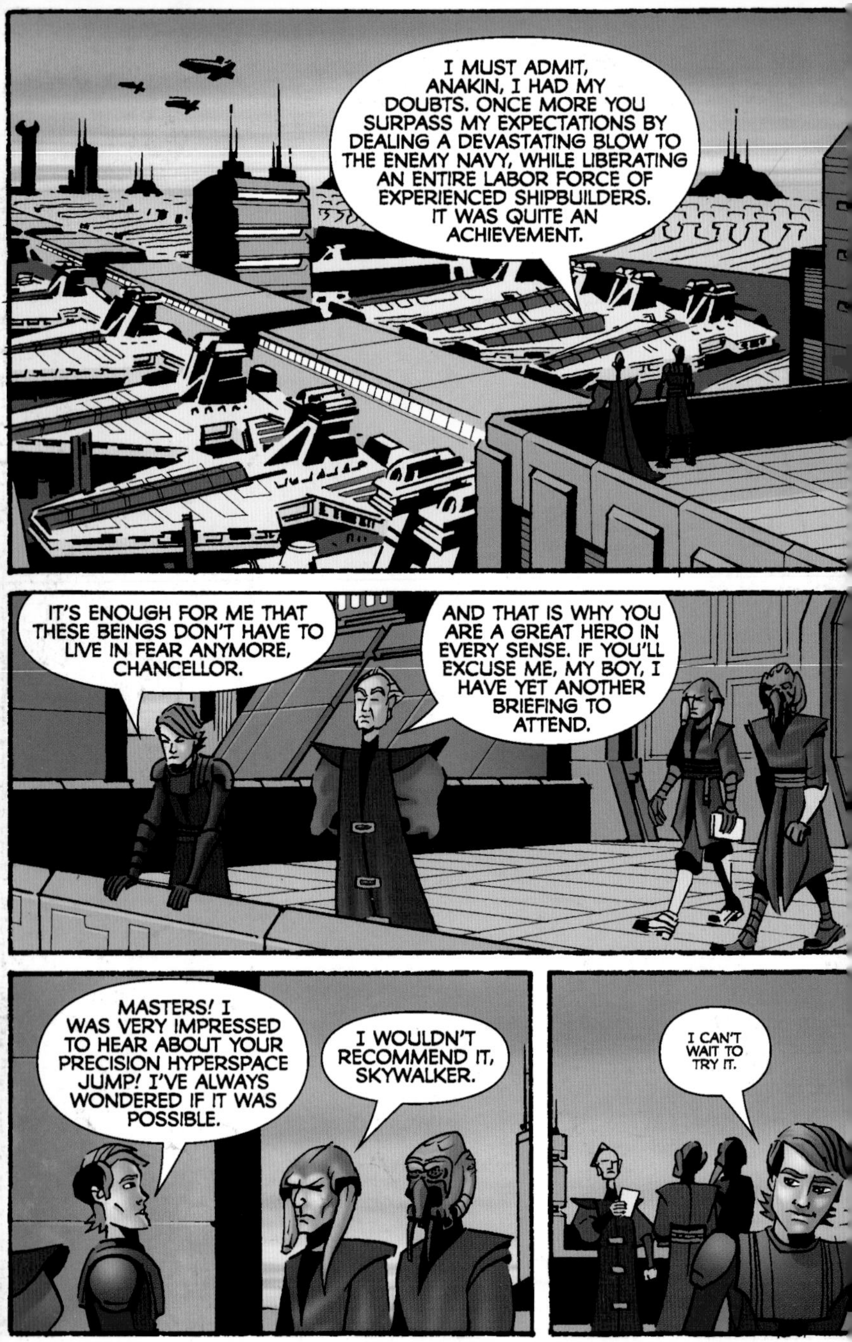
I MUST ADMIT, ANAKIN, I HAD MY DOUBTS. ONCE MORE YOU SURPASS MY EXPECTATIONS BY DEALING A DEVASTATING BLOW TO THE ENEMY NAVY, WHILE LIBERATING AN ENTIRE LABOR FORCE OF EXPERIENCED SHIPBUILDERS. IT WAS QUITE AN ACHIEVEMENT.
IT'S ENOUGH FOR ME THAT THESE BEINGS DON'T HAVE TO LIVE IN FEAR ANYMORE, CHANCELLOR.
AND THAT IS WHY YOU ARE A GREAT HERO IN EVERY SENSE. IF YOU'LL EXCUSE ME, MY BOY, I HAVE YET ANOTHER BRIEFING TO ATTEND.
MASTERS! I WAS VERY IMPRESSED TO HEAR ABOUT YOUR PRECISION HYPERSPACE JUMP! I'VE ALWAYS WONDERED IF IT WAS POSSIBLE.
I WOULDN'T RECOMMEND IT, SKYWALKER.
I CAN'T WAIT TO TRY IT.

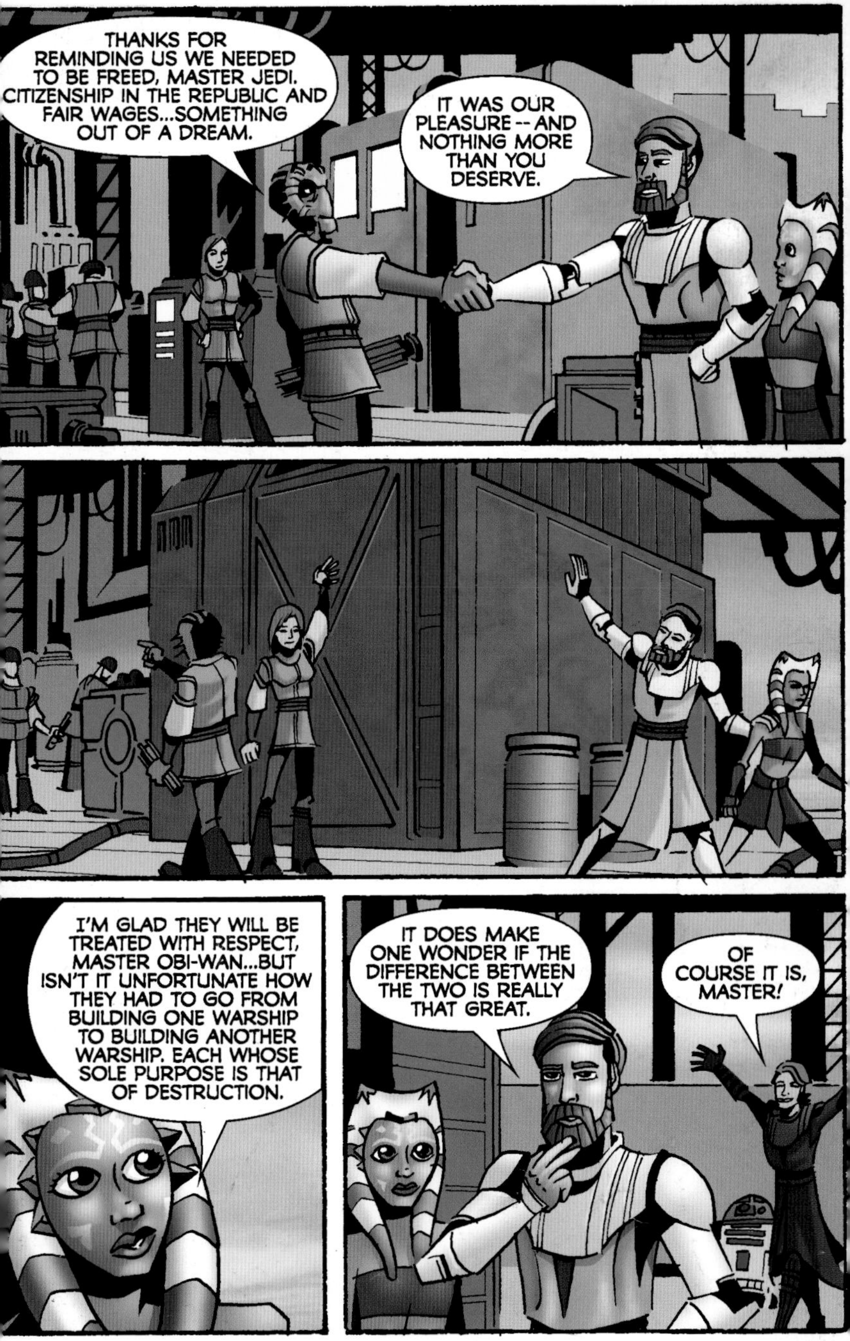
THANKS FOR REMINDING US WE NEEDED TO BE FREED, MASTER JEDI. CITIZENSHIP IN THE REPUBLIC AND FAIR WAGES...SOMETHING OUT OF A DREAM.
IT WAS OUR PLEASURE -- AND NOTHING MORE THAN YOU DESERVE.
I'M GLAD THEY WILL BE TREATED WITH RESPECT, MASTER OBI-WAN...BUT ISN'T IT UNFORTUNATE HOW THEY HAD TO GO FROM BUILDING ONE WARSHIP TO BUILDING ANOTHER WARSHIP. EACH WHOSE SOLE PURPOSE IS THAT OF DESTRUCTION.
IT DOES MAKE ONE WONDER IF THE DIFFERENCE BETWEEN THE TWO IS REALLY THAT GREAT.
OF COURSE IT IS, MASTER!

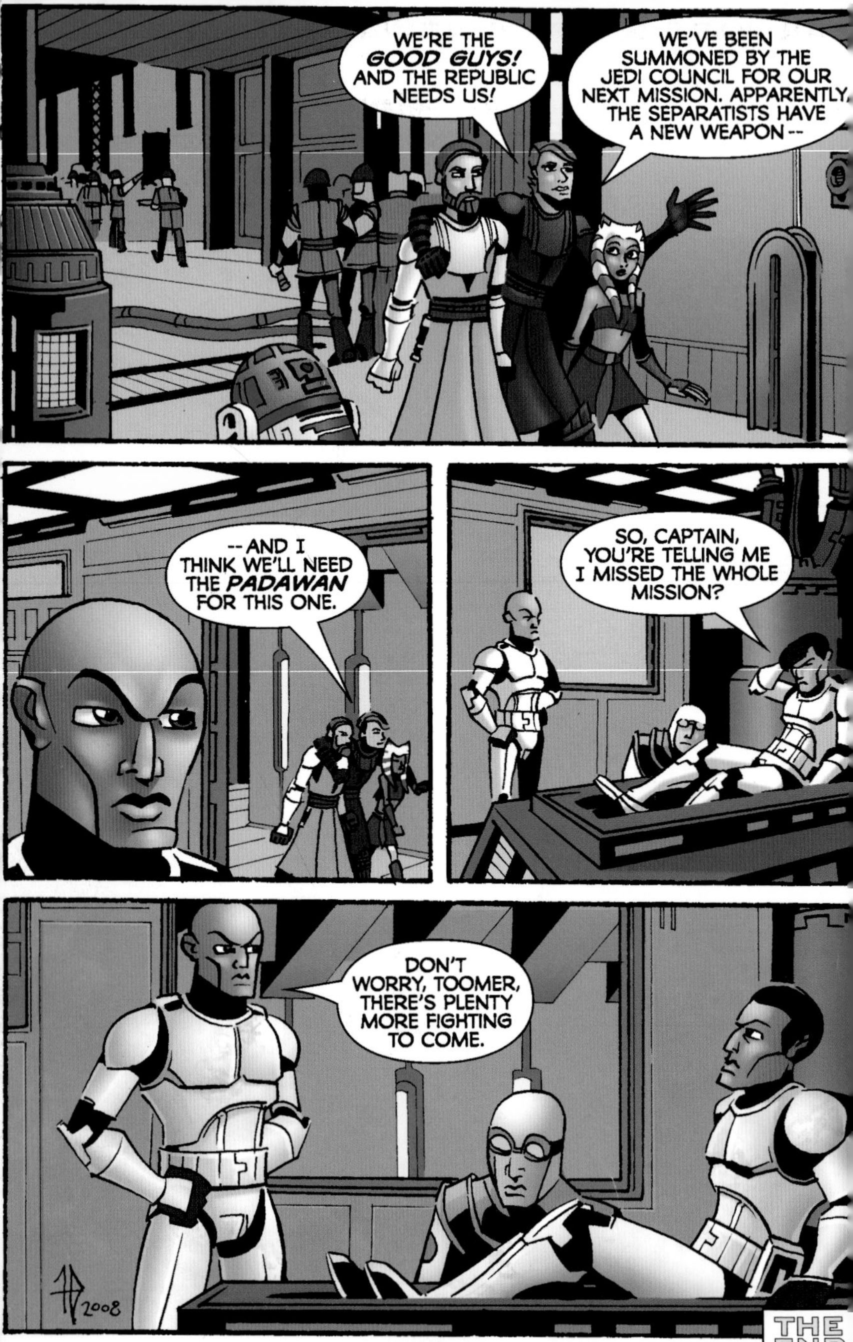
WE'RE THE GOOD GUYS! AND THE REPUBLIC NEEDS US!
WE'VE BEEN SUMMONED BY THE JEDI COUNCIL FOR OUR NEXT MISSION. APPARENTLY, THE SEPARATISTS HAVE A NEW WEAPON --
-- AND I THINK WE'LL NEED THE PADAWAN FOR THIS ONE.
SO, CAPTAIN, YOU'RE TELLING ME I MISSED THE WHOLE MISSION?
DON'T WORRY, TOOMER, THERE'S PLENTY MORE FIGHTING TO COME.
2008
THE END

TAR WARS GRAPHIC NOVEL TIMELINE (IN YEARS)

Tales of the Jedi—5,000–3,986 BSW4
Knights of the Old Republic—3,964 BSW4
Jedi vs. Sith—1,000 BSW4
Jedi Council: Acts of War—33 BSW4
Prelude to Rebellion—33 BSW4
Darth Maul—33 BSW4
Episode I: The Phantom Menace—32 BSW4
Outlander—32 BSW4
Emissaries to Malastare—32 BSW4
Jango Fett: Open Seasons—32 BSW4
Twilight—31 BSW4
Bounty Hunters—31 BSW4
The Hunt for Aurra Sing—30 BSW4
Darkness—30 BSW4
The Stark Hyperspace War—30 BSW4
Rite of Passage—28 BSW4
Jango Fett—27 BSW4
Zam Wesell—27 BSW4
Honor and Duty—24 BSW4
Episode II: Attack of the Clones—22 BSW4
Clone Wars—22–19 BSW4
Clone Wars Adventures—22–19 BSW4
General Grievous—20 BSW4
Episode III: Revenge of the Sith—19 BSW4
Dark Times—19 BSW4
Droids—3 BSW4
Boba Fett: Enemy of the Empire—2 BSW4
Underworld—1 BSW4
Episode IV: A New Hope—SW4
Classic Star Wars—0–3 ASW4
A Long Time Ago . . . —0–4 ASW4
Empire—0 ASW4
Rebellion—0 ASW4
Vader's Quest—0 ASW4
Boba Fett: Man with a Mission—0 ASW4
Jabba the Hutt: The Art of the Deal—1 ASW4
Splinter of the Mind's Eye—1 ASW4
Episode V: The Empire Strikes Back—3 ASW4
Shadows of the Empire—3–5 ASW4
Episode VI: Return of the Jedi—4 ASW4
X-Wing Rogue Squadron—4–5 ASW4
Mara Jade: By the Emperor's Hand—4 ASW4
Heir to the Empire—9 ASW4
Dark Force Rising—9 ASW4
The Last Command—9 ASW4
Dark Empire—10 ASW4
Boba Fett: Death, Lies, and Treachery—11 ASW4
Crimson Empire—11 ASW4
Jedi Academy: Leviathan—13 ASW4
Union—20 ASW4
Chewbacca—25 ASW4
Legacy—130 ASW4

Old Republic Era
25,000 – 1000 years before
Star Wars: A New Hope

Rise of the Empire Era
1000 – 0 years before
Star Wars: A New Hope

Rebellion Era
0 – 5 years after
Star Wars: A New Hope

New Republic Era
5 – 25 years after
Star Wars: A New Hope

New Jedi Order Era
25+ years after
Star Wars: A New Hope

Legacy Era
130+ years after
Star Wars: A New Hope

Infinities
Does not apply to timeline

Sergio Aragonés Stomps Star Wars
Star Wars Tales
Star Wars Infinities
Tag and Bink
Star Wars Visionaries

4 = before *Episode IV: A New Hope.* ASW4 = after *Episode IV: A New Hope.*

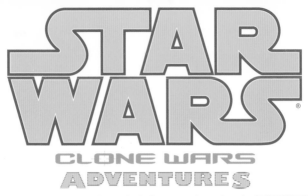

STAR WARS
CLONE WARS ADVENTURES

Don't miss any of the action-packed adventures of your favorite STAR WARS® characters, available at comics shops and bookstores in a galaxy near you!

STAR WARS
CLONE WARS
ADVENTURES
Vol 4
STAR WARS
CLONE WARS
ADVENTURES
Vol 1
THREE NEW STORIES! ALL-JEDI ACTION!
STAR WARS
CLONE WARS
ADVENTURES
Vol 10
JEDI, CLONES, DROIDS, AND BOUNTY HUNTERS IN FOUR FANTASTIC TALES!

$6.95 each!

Volume 1	ISBN: 978-1-59307-243-8
Volume 2	ISBN: 978-1-59307-271-1
Volume 3	ISBN: 978-1-59307-307-7
Volume 4	ISBN: 978-1-59307-402-9
Volume 5	ISBN: 978-1-59307-4
Volume 6	ISBN: 978-1-59307-567-5
Volume 7	ISBN: 978-1-59307-678-8
Volume 8	ISBN: 978-1-59307-680-1
Volume 9	ISBN: 978-1-59307-832-4
Volume 10	ISBN: 978-1-59307-8

AVAILABLE AT YOUR LOCAL COMICS SHOP OR BOOKSTORE

To find a comics shop in your area, call 1-888-266-4226

For more information or to order direct: • On the web: darkhorse.com • Phone: 1-800-862-0052 Mon.–Fri. 9 AM to 5 PM Pacific Time. • E-mail: mailorder@darkhorse.com *Prices and availability subject to change without notice.

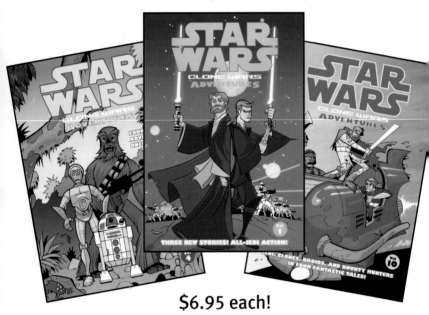